YES TO W

YES TO
WOMEN PRIESTS

edited by
HUGH MONTEFIORE

MAYHEW–McCRIMMON
in association with
A. R. MOWBRAY

© 1978 *A. R. Mowbray & Co. Ltd and
Mayhew–McCrimmon Ltd*

*First published 1978
by Mayhew–McCrimmon Ltd
10–12 High Street, Great Wakering, Essex
in association with
A. R. Mowbray & Co. Ltd,
Saint Thomas House, Becket Street, Oxford.*

ISBN 0 264 66498 1

*Typeset in 10/11 Baskerville
and printed in Great Britain
by Richard Clay (The Chaucer Press) Ltd,
Bungay, Suffolk*

CONTENTS

FOREWORD — vii

1. THE THEOLOGY OF PRIESTHOOD — 1
   The Right Rev. Hugh Montefiore, BD, HON.DD
   Bishop of Birmingham

   APPENDED NOTE
   WOMEN AND THE ORDAINED MINISTRY — 14
   Professor Donald MacKinnon, MA, HON.DD
   Norris-Hulse Professor of Divinity, Cambridge University

2. THE BIBLICAL EVIDENCE — 16
   The Rev. Christopher Evans, MA
   Professor Emeritus of New Testament Studies at King's College, London

3. MALE–FEMALE SYMBOLISM — 30
   The Rev. Canon F. W. Dillistone, DD
   Fellow Emeritus of Oriel College, Oxford

4. VOCATIONAL AND PASTORAL ASPECTS — 48
   The Rev. Canon Mary Michael Simpson, OSH
   Canon Residentiary, Cathedral Church of St John the Divine, New York

5. AN EPISCOPAL ACCOUNT OF WOMEN PRIESTS — 61
   The Right Rev. Gilbert Baker, MA
   Bishop of Hong Kong and Macao

6. WHY NOT NOW? 73
The Venerable Michael Perry, MA
Archdeacon of Durham

FOREWORD

The Anglican Communion as a whole, and the Church of England in particular, must make up its mind about the recognition of women priests from churches in full communion with the See of Canterbury; and, more importantly, the autonomous churches of the communion must make up their own minds whether or not to ordain women to the priesthood.

This book is offered as a contribution towards this question. All its contributors, men and women of standing in their own churches, believe that the time has come to ordain women and to recognize them as priests.

The argument must begin with an examination of the meaning, role and function of priesthood. For this reason the first contribution is on the theology of priesthood, together with an appended note by Professor Mackinnon on one particular aspect. Particular points of conflict centre on the interpretation of biblical evidence and the symbolic function of priesthood. Accordingly there follows an illuminating discussion of the biblical evidence by Professor Evans, and a penetrating analysis of the symbolic representation of God by Dr Dillistone. The argument here concentrates on an historical approach to symbolism, rather than on psychological analysis, because the subjective nature of the latter inevitably leads to many diverse and conflicting interpretations.

The presence of authentic vocations to priesthood by women is vital if their ordination is to be seriously considered, and there follows an account by Canon Mary Michael Simpson, OSH of her vocation and her priestly life. Important as is the interior call, its recognition by the Church is equally important, and there follows an episcopal assessment of women priests in the diocese of Hong Kong by its Bishop.

Finally, the question of expediency must be faced. Even granted that women may be ordained and that this is consonant with the theology of priesthood, what would be the effect of such a move on the other churches of Christendom? The Archdeacon of Durham meets possible objections in a final chapter entitled: 'Why Not Now?'

No doubt, if we had had more time, we could have co-ordinated our contributions more closely and produced a more considered volume. We judge however that the propinquity of the Lambeth Conference and the increasing urgency of decision-making requires from us a quick response, and we believe that in this volume we have set before our readers the heart of the matter which we hope will help them in clearing their own minds on this pressing question.

I would like to express my gratitude to Mowbrays and Mayhew-McCrimmon for accepting this manuscript at very short notice, and for all their co-operation in producing and publishing it for us.

St Anthony's Day 1978 HUGH MONTEFIORE

CHAPTER 1

THE THEOLOGY OF PRIESTHOOD

HUGH MONTEFIORE

At first sight the question of the admission of women to the Christian priesthood might seem to be merely a matter of common sense, which could be resolved in the same kind of way as their admission to other vocations and professions. But the church is not simply a human institution: it is of divine appointment. The question therefore whether women should be (or are capable of being) admitted to the priesthood depends on a theological understanding of priesthood in the church.

What is a priest? The whole church is described in scripture as a 'royal priesthood', because it is called to fulfil its vocation of self-offering to God as a living sacrifice. It is generally agreed that a priest is not only a particular representative of this 'common priesthood' but also personally called by God to enable the church to fulfil its divine vocation.[1] Christians see all priesthood as a kind of participation in Christ our high priest, who was appointed by God, empowered with indestructible life, and who offered himself in a complete and unrepeatable sacrifice.

There is a variety of images used in the New Testament to describe the functions of the Christian minister; servant, herald, ambassador, teacher, shepherd, steward and exemplar. The minister has authority in and exercises oversight over the church. So far as all these functions are concerned, they are exercised both by men and by women in the secular world. The same could be said also of the Christian Church. Fr Gerald O'Collins SJ[2] wrote in 1975 of the Roman Catholic Church:

By October 1972 German bishops had authorised 2,000 women to distribute Holy Communion at parish masses. By then about the same number enjoyed official positions as pastoral assistants in parishes and other communities.... In South America matters have gone much further than in Germany. Catholic nuns perform baptisms, preach sermons, distribute holy communion and officiate at weddings. They act as full deacons without being ordained as deacons.

Similarly there are women in positions of high responsibility in the Church of England.[3] If these functions were all that were required of a priest, then a woman could carry them out as well as a man. Perhaps because emphasis is specially laid on functional roles in Protestant churches, they have been the first to admit women as ministers.

A priest however not only has pastoral functions, as a minister of word and sacrament. He is also a representative symbol; and it is at this point that objections to women priests often arise.

Whom do priests represent? Certainly they are representatives of the church. 'They are priests', wrote R. C. Moberley[4] 'because they are personally consecrated to be the representatives and active organs of the priesthood of the Church. And they represent it emphatically in both of its directions. In the ceremonial direction they represent it as divinely empowered to be ... its leaders and instruments. And from this representative leadership.... I apprehend that it follows also, on the inward and spiritual side, that those who actually represent the Church no less specially represent it in its true inwardness.' Bishop Lightfoot, although belonging to a very different churchmanship, concurs in so far as he wrote of the Christian minister: 'His office is representative and not vicarial.' The ARCIC Agreed Statement speaks of a priest as 'representative of the whole church in the fulfilment of its priestly vocation'.[6]

Dr Packer,[7] however, holds that this representative function of priesthood does nothing to counter Dr

Demant's observation[8] that 'a male priest represents both sexes in a way which a woman does not in organised church and society' and 'men and women on the whole will not value women as representatives'. This makes strange reading in a land where a woman is the universally acclaimed and paramount representative symbol of her country. If God created male and female in his own image (Gen. 1.27; 5.1f.), either is able adequately to represent him;[9] and if there is neither male nor female, but all are one in Christ (Gal. 3.28), then—theologically speaking—either a man or a woman is an equally adequate representative of the Church.

But priests are also authorized representatives of God in Christ to the church. 'All this is from God who in Christ reconciled us to himself and gave us the ministry of reconciliation' (II Cor. 5.18). A priest stands on the Godward side of man as well as on the manward side of God. 'They exercise this sacred function of Christ most of all in the Eucharistic liturgy or synaxis. There, *acting in the person of Christ* ...'[10]

How can a woman 'act in the person of Christ'? One might as well ask, how can a Gentile act in the person of the Jewish Messiah? The official Roman Catholic answer is that 'in human beings sex exercises an important influence, much deeper than, for example, ethnic differences'.[11] To this the Editor of the Jesuit journal *The Month*[12] has responded: 'It is not Christian belief that the priest at the altar *impersonates* Jesus of Nazareth: rather he *represents* our redeemer in celebrating the sacrament of our redemption, and, in his saving significance, it seems fair to suggest that Christ's masculinity is irrelevant. What is important is the humanity which men and women share.'

In fact, the argument needs to be pressed more rigorously. The phrase 'acting in the person of Christ' needs further unpacking. The priest is not a representation of Christ: he is his representative. A priest does not represent a dead Jesus, but the risen and ascended Lord, as Roman Catholics agree. 'In the bishops, for whom priests are assistants, the supreme High Priest is present in the midst of those who believe.'[13] (As a matter of fact, Christ is present through the Spirit wherever two or three are gathered in his name; and he will remain with us until the end of the age.) In this risen Christ sex has no significance. In the resurrection, men and women 'are like the angels in heaven' (Mark 12.25). Moreover, the priest must symbolize God himself, for the Ascended Christ is the Second Person of the Blessed Trinity. And whereas the male symbolizes God as Father, Protector, Lawgiver and Judge, the female, as Dr Dillistone has so clearly demonstrated in a later chapter, is needed to represent God as Generator, Sustainer and Fulfiller of Life and Reconciler of opposites into unhindered communication.[14] It follows therefore from this theological examination of priesthood that both men and women *need* to be admitted to the priesthood.

Dr Mascall,[15] echoing the 'Undeceptions' of C. S. Lewis,[16] fears lest female participation in priesthood would result in 'a different religion', with the feminine symbols of Mother, Daughter and Bride substituted for the scriptural images of 'Our Father in Heaven', the Eternal Son made man, and the Heavenly Groom united in the nuptial mystery with the Church, his Bride. In fact these scriptural images are analogies of heavenly mysteries rather than the realities themselves. Dr Mascall's fears in any case would only be well grounded if women *alone* were to be ordained. But where men are ordained *alongside* women, the scriptural imagery of Christian revelation would continue to be symbolized in male priests, but there would be added those other profound aspects of God's saving mystery symbolized in the person of women priests.

It follows that, if priesthood is to be a fully representative sign of both Christ and the church, both men and women must be included. If the theology of priesthood is subjected to rigorous theological scrutiny it emerges that women, far from being alien to Christian priesthood, contribute to the plenitude of its expression.

If the validity of these arguments be granted, on what authority could a change of policy be effected? Anglicans recognize a threefold source of authority in Scripture, Tradition and Reason. (Reason here is used to signify the mind exercising itself beyond the sphere of bible and tradition, rather than an authority distinct from both.)

Professor Christopher Evans, in a later essay,[17] has considered the bearing of the Bible on this issue, distinguishing three possible attitudes. We may dismiss what he calls 'a text-quoting exercise'. Nothing constructive can emerge from it unless we are committed to the extraordinary belief that the Bible contains a jumbled pastiche of propositions, which, when properly ordered and juxtaposed, give authoritative directions for situations quite different from those which the writers of its constituent books could have possibly imagined.

The second approach is more critical and analytical, distinguishing those parts of Holy Scripture which show the impact of the Christian gospel from those which owe their origin elsewhere, and which may only to some extent have been brought under the gospel's influence.[18] To many (such as myself) it will seem self-evident that passages e.g. from St Paul which assert male predominance belong to the latter category; and such people will sympathize with St Paul as he struggles—not always successfully[19]—to refine the prejudices of his Jewish upbringing and the cultural assumptions of the first century with the revolutionary gospel of Christ which discloses God as no respecter of persons and as the healer of the age-old divisions of race, class and sex. But whether the exclusion of women from the apostolate in New Testament times was due to well thought out theological principles or to cultural assumptions and unavoidable practicalities, there can by the nature of the case be no *final proof*. It is rather a question for informed judgment about such fragmented and elusive evidence as may exist.

The third and most helpful approach which Professor Evans proposes is to start from the present situation with its contemporary questions—and the admission of women to the priesthood is certainly one such question—and to ask whether such a question is blocked by the gospel, or whether it is fundamentally consonant with it theologically or spiritually. In my judgment it is consonant; but here again, as Professor Evans remarks, 'stalemate is possible'. Yet he cites impressive evidence of a change of heart by leading Roman Catholic theologians, not because they now have a better understanding of the Bible but because they have been given a clearer insight into the nature of its authority.

If there is no certain reply to be had from Holy Scripture, what about the age-old tradition of the church? The churches which have preserved the historic threefold ministry of the church have not (apart from the Church of Sweden and some Anglican churches in the recent past) ordained women to the priesthood. The Vatican Declaration declares that the Fathers 'considered it as unacceptable'.[20] Fr Flusser, after a detailed examination of the texts cited, concludes that these texts 'do not bear out that contention very convincingly'.[21] Nonetheless, apart from a few heretical sects, women were not priested. In medieval times, it was the same. Certain abbesses were described as ordained, but the context suggests rather their consecration. They were mitred, given staff and ring, authorized to hear confessions, described as 'sacerdotes' and granted (for a period) ecclesiastical and civil authority.[22] These privileges however suggest episcopal jurisdiction rather than priestly orders.

How should the constant and universal past practice of the church be evaluated? There were of course undeniable prejudices against women as weak, frail, subordinate to men, the object of sexual temptation, visited with the baneful effects of the Fall and even (as St Thomas Aquinas believed) as incomplete males. These prejudices are now unacceptable. Were not these the real reasons for an exclusively male priesthood rather than the revelation of God in Christ as attested by Scripture? Professor Lampe has isolated two different types of tradition.[23] 'Part of it consists of the accumulated deposit of doctrine, the result of the constant process of formulation and explanation by which the common mind of the church has sought to interpret and reinterpret for successive generations and cultures the revelation embodied in scripture. Part on the other hand is made up of customs, the ways in which the church's life and world are organized, its worship ordered and its particular rites conducted which have grown up almost imperceptibly, have come to be taken for granted and have not usually been subjected to critical examination.' As Article XXXIV asserts, the latter type of tradition may be changed. Here again opinion divides. To some, like Professor Lampe and myself, it seems self-evident that the exclusion of women from the priesthood belongs to the latter category. But here again it is a matter not of proof but of informed judgment. The Holy Scriptures give a problematical reply to our question, and so too does tradition.

The third source of authority lies in the exercise of reason beyond the sphere of bible and tradition.

1. The first point to be made is that pronouncements on matters of sex, especially when made by an exclusively male body (above all if its members are compulsorily celibate) should be very rigorously scrutinized. (Similar comments have been made about 'Humanae Vitae' and the Vatican Declaration on Certain Questions concerning Sexual Ethics.)

2. It is worth enquiring what effect it has on an institution when women are admitted to positions of responsibility. Bishop John Taylor has noted: [24] 'It is enlightening to observe what happens to other professions when women have been admitted to them. The pattern and concept of the profession begins to undergo a process of humanization.'

3. What, it should be asked, would be the impact of women priests on their male colleagues? In other professions the result has been an enrichment as men and women have brought complementary gifts to their work. Professor C. P. Price has remarked a certain 'confusion of identity from which many clergy are suffering at the

present time'.[25] He continues: 'It is said in liberation theology that the liberation of the oppressed entails the redemption of the oppressor. In a somewhat comparable way, we could say that the ordination of women to the priesthood would be the redemption of male priests for they would be freed from the necessity of providing whatever it is that female priests might contribute to the ministry.' Incidentally, the warning being put about that women priests, as matriarchs, promote homosexuality and suicide among men shows such ignorance of anthropology and psychology (not to mention the actual situation where women have been ordained) as to appear almost pathological.[26] Irrational feelings about sex, however, can be very deeply felt. No amount of arguing will remove them. Sex for many people is a terrifying, guilt-laden department of life, to be repressed from consciousness, at least in so far as it impinges on religion and spirituality. People who may have been wounded by childhood experiences (and perhaps later affected by the assumptions of contemporary literature and the media) often think unconsciously of a woman as a sex object. For such people the idea of a woman priest is intolerable. Furthermore, the idea of women priests can arouse in both men and women a strong fear of the bisexuality which, to some degree, is inherent in human nature. For all of us the right way to deal with irrationalities about sex is not to try to reason them out of existence but to accept them for what they are, emotional 'hang-ups', which can best be dealt with not by argument but through a deeper experience of personal relationships.

4. It has already been noted that according to Judaeo-Christian tradition men and women are together made in the image of God, and possibly it is their complementarity that constitutes that image.[27] (It may also be that the biblical doctrine of the subordination of woman to man represents the result of sin and a manifestation of 'The Fall.')[28] Among the baptized, women share as fully as men in their adopted status as children of God (Gal. 3.28). Reason therefore suggests that women bring their own

distinctive gifts into the ordained ministry; and Professor Mackinnon, in an Appended Note, movingly testifies to an important aspect of that ministry which they would be able to exercise.[29]

5. There is undoubtedly a world-wide movement effecting a revolution in favour of half the human race. Article 1 of the UN Declaration about Women reads as follows: 'Discrimination against women ... constitutes an offence against human dignity.'[30] No doubt there are excesses in the sexual revolution (e.g. in aspects of the Women's Liberation Movement and in 'unisex' tendencies), but no revolution should be evaluated in terms of peripheral deviations. The solid fact emerges that modern knowledge is dispersing many ancient prejudices about women, technology and medicine are relieving them from domestic drudgery and the weakening effects of continual child-bearing and child-rearing, and we no longer have rigid stereotypes imposed upon us about their role in society. Scientific, psychological and sociological sciences combine to enable us today to see women not as identical with men, but complementary in nature and equal in status. It is hard to deny that this insight, consonant with the revelation disclosed through Jesus Christ, is due to the prompting of the Holy Spirit. It is manifested in a world-wide stirring of the human spirit. Professor Demant, however, warned against confusing 'the spirit of the age with the Holy Spirit.'[31] How are they to be distinguished? We must test our theology by its coherence and by the sources of its authority. By these criteria the views, e.g. of German Christians that under the Nazis the Volk were the new Chosen People appear hopelessly erroneous;[32] by the same criteria, the argument for admission of women to the priesthood has been tested and appears cogent and coherent.

In the secular world, there has been a call for 'women's rights'. But no one has a 'right' to be ordained. It is a calling from God. Women do however have a right for their calling to be tested. As the Report of the Doctrinal Commission of the Church in Wales has declared: [33] 'If there is a positive case for ordaining women it must be based on the existence within the church of women with a genuine vocation to the priesthood.' The testimony of the Rev. Canon Sister Mary Michael in a later chapter speaks eloquently of her genuine vocation. The Bishop of Hong Kong writes movingly of vocations in his diocese. A couple of years ago nearly a quarter of the women in full-time ministry of the Church of England indicated that they would seek ordination to the priesthood if possible.[34] There must be many more women who have never thought and prayed about their vocation to the priesthood because they have never envisaged it as a practical possibility. No doubt a fair percentage of those who believed they had vocations would not be recommended for training by a Selection Board. But that is precisely what now happens to male aspirants. I have been told by one who has to act as selector for the Church of Scotland that she has been deeply impressed by the quality of the women who offer themselves to the ordained ministry. I believe our experience in the Church of England would be similar.

Theologically speaking there ought to be a change of policy so that women could be admitted to the priesthood. The universal church has not irrevocably made up its mind on this matter. Even the Vatican Declaration is by no means final. After all, most of the criticisms of it cited in this chapter have been by *Roman Catholic* theologians.[35] As Christian Howard has noted,[36] the Anglican-Roman Catholic Agreed Statement represents the consensus of the Commission on essential matters when it considers that doctrine admits of no divergence, but the exclusion of women from the priesthood is not included among these essential matters. The Declaration itself states: 'In the final analysis, it is the Church, through the voice of her Magisterium that, in these various domains, decides what can change and what must remain immutable.'[37] The Roman Church has changed its mind on other matters and could change its mind on this issue whenever it feels guided by the Holy Spirit into a fuller apprehension of the truth. The Church of England also can and should change its mind when necessary. Such changes have in fact taken place in all churches in the fairly recent past. The most notable of these changes has been in a new understanding (after some eighteen hundred years) between authority and the inerrancy of scripture. Nor is a church to be blamed because it has not been able to see the fuller implications of the revelation in Christ until circumstances were ripe. So it was, for example, with slavery: so, pray God, it will be with the priesting of women.

But how does such a change of heart and mind take place? The Holy Spirit works in many ways; through the writings of theologians, through the responses of the faithful and the leadership of their pastors, through scientific knowledge and through world events. Gradually minds and hearts are illuminated by grace with a growing apprehension of truth.

Sometimes it is said that only an Ecumenical Council could decide a theological matter such as this. This is very doubtful. Councils are seldom theologically creative: in the past they have usually set the seal of ecclesiastical authority on theological truths already perceived.* The greatest and most far-reaching decision recognized by the Christian Church concerned the admission of Gentiles to full membership. But this was not *decided* by a Jerusalem Council in Acts 15 or earlier. The Council merely laid down the conditions under which Gentiles were expected to lead Christian lives: it *recognized* that God had already decided the question of Gentile Christians earlier by pouring out his Spirit on Cornelius. As Peter is reported to have said:

'If God gave the same gift to them as he gave to us when we believed in the Lord Jesus Christ, who was I that I could withstand God?' When they heard this, they were silenced.[38]

In the same kind of way, the ministries of Sr Mary

* See Chapter 6, p. 86.

Michael, Jane Hwang, Joyce Bennett, Pauline Shek, Mary Au (and others not cited in this book) are living witnesses to God's Spirit poured out on women admitted to the priesthood. They too should silence opposition. The evident infusion of grace in their lives and in the lives of those to whom they minister, their acceptance by their male colleagues and local congregations, the authenticity of their priestly ministry and vocation—these speak louder than words. These women are living embodiments of the theological truths which this chapter attempts to expound, and which are expanded in later chapters of this book.

NOTES

1. Cf. *Ministry and Ordination* (ARCIC Agreed Statement, 1973) para 13: *One Baptism, One Eucharist and A Mutually Recognised Ministry* (Faith and Order Paper No. 73, WCC, 1975), p. 33, paras 13f.
2. Reprinted in *Women Priests? Yes, Now!* (ed. H. Wilson, Denholm House Press, 1975), p. 46.
3. Recently during an interregnum, I placed in charge of a parish at the request of the Wardens, the Deaconess rather than one of the (far less experienced) Assistant Curates.
4. R. C. Moberley, *Ministerial Priesthood* (Murray, 1899), pp. 259f.
5. J. B. Lightfoot, *St Paul's Epistle to the Philippians* (6th ed., Macmillan, 1881), p. 267.
6. *Op. cit.*, para. 13.
7. 'Representative Priesthood,', *Why Not?* ed. M. Bruce and G. E. Duffield (Marcham Manor Press 1972), p. 80.
8. V. A. Demant 'Why the Christian Ministry is Male', *Women in Holy Orders* (Report of Archbishop's Commission, C.A. 1617, 1966), pp. 110f.
9. Professor Lampe has pointed out to me that St Thomas Aquinas located the image of God in the rational soul (mens) to which sex-differentiation does not apply.
10. Vatican II, *Lumen Gentium*, 28.
11. *Declaration on the Question of the Admission of Women to the Ministerial Priesthood* (Inter insigniores, 1977), Section V.
12. *The Month*, Second New Series, Vol. 10 No. 3 (March 1977), p. 76.
13. *Lumen Gentium*, 21.
14. See p. 47.
15. E. L. Mascall, *Women Priests?* (CLA 1972), pp. 14ff.
16. C. S. Lewis, *Undeceptions* (Bles 1971), pp. 192ff.
17. See pp. 16ff.

18. 'Interpreting the Bible is a creative process which (a) looks at a passage in the *ancient* theological, historical, cultural and linguistic context that forms the "horizon" of the writer; and (b) allows it to come alive and arrest the *modern* hearer.' (The Nottingham Statement—Official Statement of the Second National Evangelical Anglican Congress held in April 1977), p. 17.
19. E.g. 1 Cor. 11.1–16.
20. *Inter insigniores*, Section 1. The references are expanded in the official commentary.
21. M. Flusser, 'Fathers and Priestesses: Footnotes to the Roman Declaration', Worship, vol. 51 no. 5 (Sept. 1977), p. 445.
22. Cf. Joan Morris, 'Women and Episcopal Power', *New Blackfriars* vol. 53 no. 625 (May 1972), pp. 205–210.
23. 'The Church's Tradition and the Question of the Ordination of Women to the Historic Ministry of the Church' (*Evidence submitted to the Archbishop's Commission by the Anglican Group for the Ordination of Women, 1972*), pp. 1, 4f.
24. Speech in General Synod on 3 July 1975 by the Bishop of Winchester.
25. C. P. Price, 'The Argument from Theology', *Women Priests—Yes, Now!* (Denholm House Press, 1975), p. 58.
26. Reported as the view of a Suffragan Bishop interviewed by Polly Toynbee (*Guardian*, 7 October 1977).
27. Cf. Karl Barth, *Church Dogmatics*, III, 1 (T. & T. Clark, 1958), p. 196.
28. Cf. M. E. Thrall, *The Ordination of Women to the Priesthood* (SCM Press 1958), p. 35.
29. See pp. 14f.
30. *Declaration on the Elimination of Discrimination Against Women*, adopted by the UN Assembly in 1967.
31. *Op. cit.*, p. 97.
32. L. Gutteridge, *Open Thy Mouth for the Dumb* (Blackwell, 1976), cc. IV and V.
33. *Women and the Ministry* (Church in Wales Publications, 1972), p. 12.
34. In 1974, out of 329 women in full time ministry in the Church of England, 83 wished to be ordained priest (48 deaconesses, 34 licensed lay workers), 131 were uncertain, 115 said they would not seek ordination.
35. In addition those mentioned in this chapter and by Archdeacon Perry and Professor Christopher Evans, Fr Gregory Baum and Fr Charles Curran headed a list of 110 eminent RC theologians and religious writers in America who signed a petition in 1974 calling on the Roman Catholic Church to respond to 'the signs of the Spirit which are visible in our sister church'; and in 1977 members of the Faculty of the Jesuit School of Theology at Berkeley have made their objections to the Vatican Declaration

public in an Open Letter to the Apostolic Delegate (*Commonweal* (1 Apr. 1977), 204–206). J. Wijngaards (*Did Christ Rule Out Women Priests?* (Mayhew-McCrimmon 1977), p. 52) adds R. Metz, F. Klosterman, J. M. Aubert, Cardinal Danielon among others to the list of those who believe that the matter is not yet settled.
36. C. Howard, 'Ordination of Women in the Anglican Communion and the Ecumenical Debate,' *Ecumenical Review* (July 1977), p. 245.
37. *Inter Insigniores*, Section 4.
38. Acts 11.17f.

APPENDED NOTE

WOMEN AND THE ORDAINED MINISTRY

DONALD MACKINNON

In contemporary discussion among Anglicans concerning the ordination of women, there is one point which, in my judgment, has not received sufficient emphasis. It is, however, a point that, if it is to be made at all, must be made by one who is both lay in status and a male person.

We have had in recent years a great deal of discussion concerning the role of the ordained priest or minister. In all churches there have been many examples of those who have found that which they supposed irreducibly unique in their ministry, gradually diminished to vanishing point in their imagination, and their function objectively reduced to that of an amateur social worker. There have been cases of those who have in consequence either abandoned their ministry or else effectively withdrawn from it, finding satisfaction in other forms of service with or without preliminary professional training. Thus it is deeply significant that the Chairman of the Strathclyde Regional Council (Strathclyde is the largest local government unit in the United Kingdom) is a minister of the Church of Scotland, the Reverend Geoffrey Shaw, previously associated with the work of the 'Gorbals Group' of ministers and clergy in Glasgow.

I mention this many-sided discussion because I remain myself obstinately convinced that there is in the Christian ministry that which is irreducibly unique, definable indeed by reference to the mission, the death and exaltation of Jesus of Nazareth in whom the eternal Word of God is incarnate. Further I remain sufficiently committed to what is conventionally called the 'Catholic tradition' to maintain a distinctively priestly as well as pastoral and prophetic element in that ministry.

It is indeed for this reason that I wish to state out of the experience of many years that there have been, in my considered belief, occasions, some of them very important, in which a woman exercising a definitely priestly ministry, by virtue of the human perception that was hers as a woman, consecrated by her ordination, could have helped me avoid courses of action, disastrous in their outcome to myself and to others. In other words I am calling attention to the fact that where exercise of the Christian ministry in the world today is concerned, the Church of England is depriving itself of resources of deeply significant pastoral wisdom. To say that such resources are available outside the exercise of a characteristically priestly ministry is to neglect the extreme importance of availability within, for instance, the context of the very special relation between priest and penitent in sacramental confession. To write in these terms is not intended to belittle any minister or priest, from whom I have received help; it is simply to record a growing conviction, born of experience.

Further, to write in these terms is not of course to suggest that all women are suitable for the exercise of the ordained ministry any more than all men are suitable for such work. Belief in vocation may be an illusion; there must be selection. But it is greatly to be hoped that decision on this issue will be taken on grounds of principle and not on those of so-called ecumenical expediency. For what is at issue in the end may be nothing less than the fullness of effective Christian ministry in our society.

CHAPTER 2

THE BIBLICAL EVIDENCE

CHRISTOPHER EVANS

There are roughly three approaches which can be taken, and which are taken, in appealing to the Bible. There is first the text-quoting exercise. 'It says this here, therefore that', to which it is rejoined 'but it says that there, therefore this'. This method is surely doomed from the start, in so far as it rests upon a position in which all biblical statements are given equal status across the board as being biblical, whether from Old Testament or New, from law, prophet, gospel or epistle, and individual statements may be pressed for implications of a normative kind, without any accepted criterion of what is of relative authority or validity, and with no referee to rule anyone out of court. This method, or something like it, is to be found within the New Testament itself. Thus in a passage bearing closely on our subject (I Cor. 11.8f.) Paul seeks for the purpose of regulating women's dress at worship to establish doctrinally the subordinate position of women to men by an appeal to the second narrative of creation, where woman is taken out of man (Gen. 2.18–23); whereas an appeal to the first narrative of creation, that of man as man and woman alike (Gen. 1.27– in the view of some Jewish exegetes the creation of an androgynous being) could have led to a very different conclusion. It is true that not all appeals of this kind manage to stay the course, and some drop out; presumably for some reason they are judged not to be, or to be no longer, appropriate. Thus Fr J. N. M. Wijngaards in his extended pamphlet, which is a critique of the *Declaration on the Question of the Admission of Women to the Ministerial Priesthood* issued with commentary by the Sacred Congregation for the Doctrine of the Faith in January 1977, remarks that two of the previous traditionalist arguments from scripture do not appear in this document, the argument that as in scripture God is always spoken of as male the human male is a better image of deity and representative of God in worship, and the argument that in scripture woman is by divine decree subjected to man as the head of the family and *a fortiori* head in matters of religion.[1] Nevertheless, the Bible is so large and diverse that some of the texts treated in this way are bound to be in contradiction, and from this method of using them there is no other possibility than stalemate. And stalemate means that what has hitherto occupied the field in a particular Christian tradition continues to do so.

The second approach is a critical one; that is, it is analytical and discriminatory. It aims to bring to light as clearly as is possible the circumstances, conditions and contexts in which something was said and done, and if possible to establish what is closer to, or the more immediate creation of, what the gospel is understood to be, as compared with what has been taken over from elsewhere and, perhaps, only partly brought under the impact of the gospel. The following example may be quoted from the conclusion of such an analysis and discrimination in an allied subject from a paper by the Swiss scholar Willy Rordorf on *Marriage in the New Testament and in the Early Church*.

> There is a whole area of marriage morality, which, it would seem to me, is not really derived from the essence of the Christian Gospel. It is found, to be sure, in the New Testament, but its sources are not so much to be found in the message of Jesus or any of his apostles as in the general environment of the classical world. This area of New Testament ethics is often referred to by the German word *Haustafeln*, that is, those lists of laws for the family and the running of the house which we might simply call domestic duties.
>
> These lists of domestic duties reflect the social structures and the rules of good conduct of the age.

The Christian message is not interested in changing them. Rather it teaches the Christian to live 'in the Lord' within the ordinary framework of his culture. It is among these relations between civil authorities and ordinary citizens, between master and slave, between parent and child, that we find the ideal for the relationship of man and wife, and this relationship is stated in about the same terms as we find in post-exilic Judaism.... In all the various versions of these lists of domestic duties, both in biblical and patristic literature, we find that a woman's submission to her husband is the central theme. What is amazing is how this aspect of classical culture has so unsuspectingly been drawn into the Christian tradition. The apostle Paul even makes an attempt to base woman's submission on an anthropological argument. In I Cor. xi he tries to prop up the rather curious dictum that women must wear veils in church. According to Paul man is made in the image of God while woman is a reflexion of man. But one almost senses that Paul is as uncomfortable with his argument as we are. This is especially evident when he says, 'Nevertheless in the Lord woman is not independent of man nor man of woman; for woman was made from man, so man is now born of woman' (I Cor. xi.11–12). This remark obviously weakens his whole argument.[2]

Rordorf then goes on to say that he is not criticizing, in the sense of sitting in judgment upon, the early church for having uncritically adopted the social structures and patterns of conduct of its environment, and he says why; but then he states conclusions in respect of the present. 'The new social structures will need a new set of Christian ethics and a new Christian social criticism. It would be anachronous to try to realise some ethical standards of New Testament times in the twentieth century. Worse than an anachronism it would be an inhuman legalism, and that certainly was not the intention of the exhortations of the first Christians. In our society it would make no sense to preach the obedience of slaves to their masters.

In fact, if anyone were to try it we would consider his preaching intolerable. It is the same with the submission of women to their husband's.'[3]

Here is an attempt to analyse and to discriminate in what is a kindred subject to our own—and it may be noted that the lists of duties to which Rordorf refers, while in Ephesians, Colossians and I Peter they are limited to the relationships of husband and wife, parents and children, masters and slaves, are extended in the Pastoral Epistles to cover ministers in the church. This approach does not end with analysis and discrimination, but makes an attempt to discern what is primary, in the sense of being closer to what is judged to be the creative core of the gospel, and what is secondary in relation to what has been judged primary, and so to assign relative degrees of authority. The approach is, however, undeniably difficult to sustain, and it will be vulnerable at many points. Quite apart from the problem of distinguishing between what one chooses to call analysis and discrimination and a superior attitude to others who do not see it that way, it is only successful to the extent that the successive steps of the analysis carry conviction as they are being made, and that deductions drawn from material which is often fugitive in character and full of lacunae are granted as the most likely explanations of the evidence at hand. And it is never able to establish an authority like that of an inspired, inerrant scripture. It is, nevertheless, how the majority of biblical scholars do in fact work, and feel themselves compelled to work, in the conviction that, whatever its faults and limitations, this approach answers to the nature of scripture itself, and brings to light more clearly the character of scriptural statement.

For what would seem often to emerge from analysis of this kind are situations in the early church where thought is still in movement, where there is tension arising from various sources, and not only between persons or groups but in the same person. This is especially evident in Paul, whose epistles in fact provide the bulk of the evidence from which the early development of the church, at least in some areas, may be glimpsed. Thus in Gal. 3.28

Paul asserts as the consequence of the gospel, and of the justification, faith, baptism and divine sonship which proceed from it, that 'there is neither Jew nor Greek, there is neither slave nor free, there is neither male nor female; for you are all one (man) in Christ Jesus'. This is an assertion in principle of an unparalleled equality and freedom over against the racial, social and sexual distinctions which obtained in the world, including the Jewish world from which the gospel had come. There are no first or second class believers. But this equality was 'in Christ'; that is, it was an eschatological fact belonging to the new world and the new creation heralded by Christ, already glimpsed by virtue of what Christ was and is, and in some sense a present reality. In what sense, however, and with what practical consequences for the life of the Christian and of the Christian communities in the racial, social and sexual spheres, had still to be discovered and worked out. And in this working out the same eschatological perspective could operate in a different direction. Thus, in I Cor. 7, where Paul is engaged in working it out in the particular circumstances of the Christian community at Corinth, it is the nearness of the end (7.29), and the consequent conviction that the present world order was on the point of passing away (7.31) which prompt the judgment that the Christian should remain in that state of life in which he had been called—if a Jew a Jew, if a Gentile a Gentile, if a slave a slave (no mention is made of masters), if unmarried then unmarried so far as was possible, and if married then married except in certain conditions of a mixed marriage. There is evidently here considerable tension. On the one hand the distinctions between male and female held to have been established at creation, and those between Jew and Gentile and between free and slave brought about in history, are annulled in the sphere of salvation. 'There is, then, in the eschatological community of Christ no longer a person whose primary characteristic is woman nor any person whose primary status is man'.[4] On the other hand, these distinctions do not themselves belong within the sphere of salvation but to the sphere of the world, and the institutions they have brought about are those of a passing world and are spiritually irrelevant.

But even here there are differences. Of the three areas concerned, the racial, social and sexual, Paul, in the first, the relation of Jew and Gentile, does draw conclusions of a practical kind such as to challenge and change the existing order, and to give effect in the present to the new humanity in Christ. For whatever concessions he may have made in the particular instances of Timothy (Acts 16.3), of Titus (? Gal. 2.3), or of the apostolic decree (Acts 15.29—the matter is not clear), he opposed all those, including Peter himself, who demanded some measure of Jewishness, and the food rules which went with it, as a necessary part of the Christian way of life, as betraying the freedom of Christ; and as a consequence in his apostolic and evangelistic practice he brought about an actual equality between Jew and Gentile as fellow workers which was to become part of the permanent structure of the whole church. In the relationship of men and women, on the other hand, while he enunciates in his instructions on marriage 'in the Lord' a mutuality and equality of rights and responsibilities which are in marked contrast with the doctrine of male dominance which obtained elsewhere, especially in Judaism—it is the judgment of the American scholar W. Meeks that 'Paul presupposes and approves in the Corinthian congregation an equivalence of role and a mutuality of relationship between the sexes in questions of marriage, divorce, and charismatic leadership of the church to a degree that is virtually unparalleled in Jewish or pagan society'[5] —he is unable to carry this through consistently, and is on occasions prepared to fall back on conventions and customs based upon this doctrine. Similarly, while in the personal instance of the slave Onesimus, which the letter to Philemon has preserved to us, Paul may be requesting (though not ordering) that the returned slave be given his freedom as a Christian brother (Philemon

16), he evidently saw no need to generalize from this and to require the abolition of the institution of slavery as such, even within the Christian community. The problem of interpretation here, if the interpreter is not content simply with as adequate an analysis and exegesis as possible of what Paul once said and why he was led to say it, but is looking for authoritative guidance from Paul for Christian decision in the present, is where the emphasis is rightly to be placed. Since we do not, and with the best will in the world cannot, share the identical eschatological position and perspective of Paul, and when the social and sexual structures of our society may be significantly different, is it his particular judgments in bringing these together which are prescriptive, or is it rather his theological vision of the new humanity in Christ and the fact that in his own time he knew himself to be committed to a struggle to give effect to it?

These problems, with additional difficulties besides, obtain in the only New Testament passage which could be said to deal with the question of women ministers in the church—and even there the bearing may be indirect. This is the discussion of various aspects of Christian worship as it was taking place in Corinth which occupies chapters 10 to 14 of I Corinthians. There is first the statement in 11.5: 'But any woman who prays or prophesies with her head unveiled dishonours her head.' The unavoidable implication of this statement is that women in Corinth took such a public part in the Christian assembly at Corinth as went with the exercise of the gift of prophecy—whatever that may have been and involved. As C. K. Barrett comments: 'The verse is meaningless unless women were from time to time moved, in the Christian assembly in Corinth, to pray and prophesy aloud and in public (not simply in family prayers and other small groups—Bachmann). If moreover Paul had thought it wrong for them to do so he would certainly not have wasted time in discussing what, in these circumstances, they should do with their heads; he would simply have forbidden the practice.'[6] Whether it is the Lord's Supper that is under consideration throughout chapters 10–14 and this prayer and prophesying took place in the context of its celebration, or the Supper only begins to be considered at 11.17 and the prayer and prophesying belongs to a separate service of the word, is a matter of debate.[7] Even if the latter were the case, it would probably be an anachronism to make a clear distinction between sacrament and word, as later came to be done, sometimes with the implication that the service of the word was in some way less representative of Christian worship than the sacrament. Whether the prophecy by women—or by anyone—would properly be called a 'ministry' exercised by 'ministers' depends on the sense in which these terms are being used. In the light of I Cor. 12.4–29 it would appear that prophecy was one ministry amongst others, but the epistle itself provides no evidence for judging whether there was at Corinth a 'ministry' in what became the more normal meaning of the term, i.e. a presbyteral ministry, or whether one or other of the presbyters 'presided' at the Eucharist, or what the relation might have been between such ministers and prophets. The argumentation upon which Paul embarks in 11.2–16 to lay a theological foundation, along with appeals to custom, for the subordinate place of women is not, then, made in order to remove the right of prophecy from them but to regulate it, perhaps to prevent its becoming an occasion for the assertion of emancipation as such. But this latter point is not clear, as it is also not clear whether the veiling of women to which he appeals is a Greek custom which the Corinthian women are repudiating, or a universal custom, or a Jewish custom which had either been introduced along with their conversion to Christianity or was now being introduced by Paul for the first time at Corinth.[8] Dr M. D. Hooker expounds the obscure—and in the course of the argument unexpected—statement of 11.10: 'For this reason a woman ought to have authority (exousia—one would have expected "veil" here) on her head because of the angels' to mean that the veil is to be worn not as a sign of her subordination to man, but rather as a sign, both that in worship she is no longer simply reflecting the glory of man, as she does when unveiled, and also that as declaring God's word in prophecy she has authority and power from God.[9] Finally, at the end of this whole section on the conduct of Christian worship at Corinth comes the injunction in 14.34f.: 'The women should keep silence in the churches. For they are not permitted to speak, but should be subordinate, as even the law says. If there is anything they desire to know, let them ask their husbands at home. For it is shameful for a woman to speak in church.' This stands in plain contradiction to 11.5, and the various attempts to avoid the contradiction are special pleading.[10] Barrett sees only two possible explanations; the first, which on balance he prefers, that these verses are a marginal note written in the spirit of the Pastoral Epistles (cf. I Tim 2.11f.) and incorporated into the text, the second, that Paul has been informed of an outbreak of female loquaciousness peculiar to Corinth, and he disciplines it in the same way as he had disciplined the male prophet over length of speech (14.30). There is plainly here much to try the patience of the commentator, and Barrett aptly appends here a comment of Calvin on this last passage, which could apply to others also: 'The discerning reader should come to the decision, that the things which Paul is dealing with here are indifferent, neither good nor bad; and that they are forbidden only because they work against seemliness and edification.'[11] To which, however, it could be added that what is seemly and edifying in one context can in a changed situation become unseemly and unedifying.

It is partly as a result of the frequently inconclusive results of an analytical approach—inconclusive generally because the character of the material does not allow otherwise—that there emerges a third type of approach to the Bible as a court of appeal in matters of Christian faith and life. This approach is to start from what is immediately in front of one and presses for recognition, or from what a considerable number of those whose judgment one trusts feel, or one feels oneself, to be urgent in respect of Christian life and thought, and then to ask the questions whether there is anything in scriptural statement which stands in its way, blocks it or rules it out; whether there is anything which is to be judged deeply rooted theologically and spiritually in the Bible which says that this is not right; and whether what appears to stand in the way does so because it is deeply rooted in the theology and spirituality of the Bible or because it is deeply rooted in the particular cultural environments in which the biblical revelation has taken place.

It is from within this approach that two of the arguments most commonly advanced are probably to be considered. There is the argument, firstly, that the choice by Jesus of only men for his apostles was a deliberate act having as part of its intention to rule out women as possible representative ministers in the church he was founding, and secondly the fact that the incarnation of God took place in a Son establishes as from the mind of God himself that he is to be represented incarnationally and sacramentally only by the man. These are arguments peculiarly difficult to assess. Evidently for some who are concerned with the matter they constitute the heart of it, but they also bring to light the widest possible divide. For to those who are convinced by them they tend to appear self-evident and decisive, with the authority of God behind them, while to those not so convinced they tend to appear as having little or no cogency, and as somewhat ludicrous in their claim to a deductive knowledge of the inner workings of God.

The second of the two arguments is strictly speaking doctrinal rather than scriptural, and in its own terms admits of being stood on its head. For it could be argued that if incarnation is really to be incarnation it involves as a necessary consequence a commitment by God to whatever conditions of life and thought are prevalent at the time and place concerned, of which male dominance in all matters might happen to be one. A doctrine of incarnation in any form is bound to bring with it the questions whether, when, and how a line is to be drawn between what is essential to the divine truths which are to be conveyed to men and what is relative and contingent in the conveying of those truths. 'God's Word became human in its forms of expression. Teasing out the divine message from the form in which it was embedded is not always easy. But it is absolutely essential in theology. The question whether some word or deed is intentional, or only part of the framework, spells life or death for theological meaning.'[12]

This is what is involved, though now with a more specifically scriptural reference, in the first argument, that concerning Jesus and his choice of the apostles. There are, of course, a whole cluster of problems attached to this, at least when it is advanced in what has been the more traditional form that the choice of the twelve was the appointment by Jesus for a future universal church of apostles as foundation ministers, whose function was to be continued in an apostolic succession of bishops along with presbyters and deacons. For whether and in what form Jesus envisaged a 'church', whether he himself named the twelve 'apostles' as Luke asserts (Luke 6.13), what the choice of the twelve signified in relation to the rest of his mission and work—the only statement about them from his lips during his earthly ministry is that they were as a body to be ('in the new world', Matt. 19.28, 'at my table in my kingdom', Luke 22.30) the eschatological co-judges of the (twelve) tribes of Israel—what the relation was between this function and the universal mission to which they are represented as having been committed through the resurrection, and what actual part they played as a body in the early life and development of the church—all these have been, and still are, hotly debated questions, and in view of the character of the New Testament evidence are inevitably so. Nevertheless, though these problems may somewhat blunt the edge of the argument in its more traditional form, they do not dispose of it. For there was presumably some connection, even if we cannot say precisely what, between the choice of the twelve by Jesus in the course of his mission on the one hand and the resultant church and its ministry on the other; and the question may still be asked whether this original choice was intentionally a male one, and as such prescriptive in the early church when it came to create a ministry, or whether in both cases it was male because the culture of the time, whether Palestinian or Graeco-Roman, did not allow of any other and precluded that any other should even be entertained. But the problem then is, how could we possibly know the answer to such questions?

Certainly the evidence that society in Palestine, and in most other places, was orientated upon the man as father, husband, owner and natural leader in all things is overwhelming. Judaism was a heavily male religion, with the woman having a secondary and derivative position. It could hardly have been otherwise when the superiority of the man was so deeply embedded in the religious tradition, so far as mankind itself was concerned in the stories of creation, and so far as Israel was concerned in the stories of the founder figures, the patriarchs (the word is significant; could those who were to judge the twelve tribes thus founded be other than men?), in the story of salvation in the Exodus and in a multitude of ways in the Law which had proceeded from it, in judges and prophets (with Deborah a solitary exception), priests and wise men, up to the priests, scribes and rabbis of the first century AD. In the circumstances to have appointed women to a representative position in the 'true' Israel that was being created would have involved simultaneously, and over and above whatever was intended by appointing a ministry, a gigantic revolution in the accepted pattern of things.

It is, perhaps, the force of these considerations which has led the authors of the recent Roman Catholic document on the matter, to which reference has already been made, to juxtapose the choice of the apostolate by Jesus and the gospel evidence concerning his attitude to women, to argue from the latter that it shows him as by no means simply conforming to social custom but on the contrary as departing widely from it, and by this route to reach the conclusion that in the face of such a revolutionary attitude towards women his limitation of the apostolate to men must have been deliberate and intentional, and therefore doctrinally authoritative. Again the argument, even in this fresh form, is difficult to assess. It may well be that scattered elements in the gospel picture, especially the Lukan gospel picture, do bespeak an attitude to women very significantly different from what is known of rabbis, prophets, preachers, religious leaders—or whatever category Jesus is to be placed in for the purpose of comparison here—in first-century Judaism. Fr Wijngaards, in rebutting this form of argument, probably goes too far in the other direction in claiming that all the instances of Jesus' dealing with women come under the head of the exercise of compassion without raising the question of women as such at all, especially as later he admits that the Lukan picture in the gospel and in Acts calls for some explanation, and himself offers the explanation that Luke sought to teach that new developments were to be expected in the church, which developments were implicitly contained in Jesus' actions and words.[13] But whether the evidence, such as it is, can bear the heavy probative weight that is being put upon it here, and can be used as a foil to establish as proven the deliberate and intentional character of the limitation of the apostolate to men, is another matter. Along this line also it would appear that stalemate is possible, and again because the material of the gospels is not of such a kind as to permit of certain answers to this type of question. As Fr Y. Congar has put it in his personal testimony: 'I would simply say that, to my view, the prohibition of the feminine priesthood is not of divine law. But I add: what authorises one to say that this restriction is only of a socio-cultural nature? I deny that one can say this with absolute certainty.'[14]

It is the case, however, that there are theologians for

whom this argument against the ministry of women in the church has once been powerful and valid, but who have come to abandon it. What has happened when such a view is abandoned and no longer held to be valid? It is not that a different conclusion is reached on the basis of a fresh appreciation of the authority of individual texts, or of a series of texts, or that a new analysis of what is primary and what secondary has become decisive. What is generally involved is a kind of conversion of attitude towards the scriptures, to what they are authoritative for and in what way they are authoritative. And this can result in a statement as precise as that of Karl Rahner when he writes: 'The practice which the Catholic Church has of not ordaining women to the priesthood has no binding theological character.... The actual practice is not a dogma. It is purely and simply based on a human and historical reflection which was valid in the past in cultural and social conditions which are presently changing rapidly.'[15]

NOTES

1. *Did Christ Rule Out Women Priests?* (Mayhew-McCrimmon, 1977), pp. 19f.
2. *Journal of Ecclesiastical History*, vol. XX, 1969 pp. 198f.
3. *Ibid.*, p. 199.
4. R. Scroggs, 'Paul and the Eschatological Woman', *Journal of the American Academy of Religion*, vol. 41, 1972, p. 288.
5. 'The Image of the Androgyne: Some Uses of a Symbol in Earliest Christianity', *History of Religions*, vol. 13, no. 3, 1974, pp. 199f.
6. *The First Epistle to the Corinthians* (Adam & Charles Black, 1968), p. 250
7. H. Conzelmann, *I Corinthians* (Fortress Press, 1975), p. 182.
8. Conzelmann, *op. cit.*, pp. 184–186.
9. 'Authority on Her Head: An Examination of I Cor. 11.10', *New Testament Studies*, vol. X, 1963, pp. 410–416.
10. Conzelmann, *op. cit.*, p. 246.
11. Barrett, *op. cit.*, pp. 332f.
12. Wijngaards, *op. cit.*, p. 46.
13. *Op. cit.*, pp. 35f and 73ff.
14. Cited by Wijngaards, *op. cit.*, p. 52.
15. Cited by Wijngaards, *op. cit.*, p. 53.

CHAPTER 3

MALE–FEMALE SYMBOLISM

F. W. DILLISTONE

Priests, priestesses, prophets, prophetesses, pastors, preachers have without exception been individuals acting in representative capacities. They have acted at particular times and places on behalf of particular communities to which they have belonged. In so acting they have adopted *symbolic* roles, for all symbols are designed to bring together *two* entities—two objects, two events or two situations. A symbolic person, through actions and character, brings together an individual or a community to which he is related and some other quality or person beyond immediate experience.

The essential function of symbols is to extend human experience and knowledge and this means that sooner or later certain highly important questions arise. Can symbolic persons be found who can act on the one hand as representatives of their community and on the other hand—and simultaneously—as representatives of ultimate reality? Or again can symbolic individuals bring together their community in its present existence with events of universal significance which have happened in the past or are expected to happen in the future? Put quite simply can symbolic persons bring us into relation with personal presence and action transcending the boundaries of space and time? This is, I judge, the basic question at the root of all other questions about ministry and priesthood.

I

Let us begin with certain assumptions about the social organization of mankind which seem now to have gained general acceptance. It appears that many communities have succeeded in finding the necessary means for their subsistence within strictly limited areas. They have been relatively independent of external change and the range of their communal experience has, in consequence, been entirely circumscribed.

The constant uncertainty within all such communities has been that of the preservation and renewal of *life* itself. None could escape from physical death. The struggle to survive in face of disease and natural ills was unremitting. The threat of infertility in the womb and in nature could never be ignored. Unless there existed in some mysterious realm perpetual sources of renewed vitality the human condition seemed hopeless. In the organization of society the role of highest distinction was that of the symbolic mediator of *life*, representing the outstanding social need and bringing it into effective relationship with some supra-human source of supply.

The many variations of this general pattern need not detain us for it has gained what might be called archetypal expression within the immensely impressive structure of social organization which developed as a result of the discovery of regular methods of agriculture. The fecundity of mother-earth, coupled with its dependence upon adequate water supplies; the seemingly miraculous process by which seed buried in the soil produced sprouts of fresh green; the possibilities of preserving grain in store-houses and of binding the whole society together as its varying members performed their appointed tasks; all this brought about a new era in the history of mankind, an era rejoicing in a host of new symbolic forms, above all in the realm of religious imagery.

In this concern for continuing life it was inevitable that the focus of practical interest should have been the land, the mysterious source of life-energies. The symbolic representation of the ultimate bestower of the bounty by which all life was sustained took the form of Earth-Mother, whose worship constitutes the dominant feature of the religion of the ancient Mediterranean world. And just as the human mother needed in some way to be impregnated and sustained, (ages passed before the dawning of any general awareness of the dependence of generation upon the sexual act) so too the earth-mother had to be provided with a continuous supply of those elements which would enable her to generate and sustain life. Symbolic agents offered symbolic gifts—water, grain, fruit, blood—but at all times one fundamental principle governed the ritual drama. It was the principle of *sacrifice*. Through some form of symbolic offering, some form of symbolic death, new potencies would be engendered and the continuance of the life of the society would be ensured.

Over a period covering thousands of years no uniformity of ritual observances can be identified nor any restriction of cult-officials to one or other of the sexes. Yet the dominating note of the ancient agricultural economies was reverence for the feminine. The earth-mother was the divinity held in deepest awe and esteem. Cult-agents were normally priestesses. The motif of cult-actions was pre-eminently the continuance of fertility and fruitfulness. Male deities and male officiants had significant tasks to perform but behind all was a sustained devotion to the land and the conviction that only through some form of sacrificial action could its fecundity be preserved.

Yet although the most noteworthy development of human experience and organization during some ten millennia has been the building up of civilizations upon the foundation of an agricultural economy—sowing, planting, irrigating, harvesting, distributing, storing—and although within these civilizations communal ritual-forms have been directed towards the generating and sustaining and ordering of *life*, life which seemed in a mysterious way to depend upon the fruitfulness of the feminine, whether amongst animals and humans or the earth itself, it is clear that this was not the exclusive form of early social organization. Far back in the past there had been tribes of hunters and there have never ceased to be societies whose pattern of life has been nomadic rather than settled, migratory rather than cyclic. Even when the notable advance was made by which animals were tamed and made subservient to man's more regular needs, the urge to be on the move was never extinguished. There was the continuing search for water and fresh pasture, for new possibilities of exchange, even simply for a better habitat.

In societies of this kind the dominating concert has ever been the discovery of fresh sources of *energy* and their exploitation. In the struggle with wild beasts and hard natural conditions the all-important factors were superior strength and skill, co-operation and loyalty. The women tended the fire and supervised the family and the camp but it was the man who was responsible for the food-supply and protection. When carrying or suckling a child, a woman was incapable of hunting or fighting. Occasionally a woman leader might appear but this was a rarity. The whole economy depended upon the strength and the purpose of the male. In such a society the land is of little concern except as an imagined far-off haven of rest. Men seek the aid of divinities believed to be strong and active on their behalf. The all-important mediator between the tribe and its special deity is the man inspired by a powerful divine spirit and capable of discerning and communicating divine directions for the advancement of the tribe's interests.

In all situations in which the dominant concerns have been superior physical strength and directions for its effective use in future enterprises, men have inevitably gained pre-eminence on the public plane. Behind the scenes women have had essential tasks to perform but these have been regarded as secondary. For the welfare of the community man's strength and skills have been of primary significance and he too has been the symbolic link with transcendent power and wisdom. Those who have chosen to journey to and fro on barren steppes or on the high seas have consistently sought the aid of a Strong Deliverer and of a Foreseeing Leader. The hero and the prophet have been the archetypal symbolic figures in the religious activities of dynamic societies.

II

It has been a comparatively simple matter to isolate these two distinctive patterns of early social organization. The polarity between the structure of a society based upon the soil and the regular cycle of the seasons on the one hand and that determined by the struggle with elemental forces and the challenge of unfamiliar conditions on the other is obvious. It is much more difficult to analyse social and religious patterns of behaviour when societies began to come into vital contact with one another and even to intermingle.

No more vivid example of this intermingling of the nomad and the land-based can be found than in the records of the Old Testament. The Canaanites, the settled inhabitants of Palestine, were agriculturalists. They grew wheat and barley: they gathered harvests of grapes and figs and olives. They celebrated festivals to mark the seasons and they regularly offered sacrifices at local shrines. Amongst many deities the goddess Asherah occupied pride of place.

In contrast, the pilgrim people from the wilderness had never been free from anxieties about food and water and their place of encampment. They kept a weekly day of rest and celebrated an annual spring festival. Their leader was a prophet believed to be the mouth-piece of the God Yahweh who in turn was conceived as Shepherd and Ruler of his people.

The Old Testament writings are now generally regarded as having originated from the period after the arrival of the tribes in Canaan and therefore as giving direct evidence of the fluctuations between assimilation and exclusiveness which characterized Israel's history for many centuries. That there were many who settled on the land and gradually accommodated themselves to the established ritual practices seems certain. Yet the strongest and most enduring policy was that which took over elements of the agrarian social organization and ritual practice and made them subservient to the kingship of Yahweh and to the worship of the people whom he had brought into covenant relationship with himself. A social hierarchy was set up under an earthly king: a system of regular festivals and sacrifices was established under an organized priesthood. Again and again attempts were made to accommodate Israel entirely to the local nature-religion and to make continuing *life* within a settled hierarchical *order* the ultimate concern. But just as often prophetic reformers were at hand to recall the people to the living God and to his acts of saving power, to his covenant which transcended all other forms of social organization and to his revealed purpose which must govern social behaviour.

Does this mean that the figure of Yahweh as conceived in the Old Testament is depicted through an exclusively male symbolism? It has been pointed out that when Israel is referred to as a son or a child the imagery is as often that of a mother's care as it is of a father's guidance. But the use of this imagery is quite rare. The symbolic titles constantly employed in reference to Yahweh are Shepherd, King, Warrior, Deliverer—all concerned with the male responsibility to act strongly for the defence, guidance and welfare of those committed to his charge. The mother-son symbolism is not entirely absent but the most striking use of sexual imagery depicts the role of Yahweh as husband to his covenant people. The bond which has been established between them is comparable to a commitment in marriage but it is Israel which is likened to the feminine partner.

The most puzzling use of feminine symbolism is to be found in the Wisdom literature where Wisdom, the agent of Yahweh, is personified as a woman. This may be partly explained by the fact that the Hebrew word translated wisdom is feminine in gender but it seems doubtful that this alone would have legitimized the creation of so impressive a female symbol. The literature belongs to a period when Israelites were increasingly in contact with other nations and when Egypt, in particular, was developing systems of general education. There were instructresses in schools and mothers in the home interested themselves in teaching the way of life. In the biblical passages Wisdom is clearly subordinate to Yahweh: she is agent and attribute. But the feminine role as begetter and fashioner is certainly celebrated and the role of woman as artist and teacher is at least envisaged.

III

The key question now arises: how did the generally accepted view of the relationship between the sexes affect the early Christian movement's symbolic forms of expression (in language, in ritual forms, in the ordering of communal life) as they appear first in a Jewish and then in a Graeco-Roman context? The witness to the life, death and resurrection of Jesus was the life-force of the new movement. It had to be expressed through symbolic forms already treasured by particular communities.

In the case of Judaism, there can be no doubt about its patriarchal character. The patriarchs, the prophet Moses, the king David, the priest-scribe Ezra were its representatives a mediators of the Covenant. Within the covenant-relationship God had made himself known as Elector, Protector, Law-giver, Judge, Guide. At the beginning of the Christian era the altogether central feature of Judaism was its worship of the God who had revealed the true and only way of life through the Law. The official teachers and interpreters of the Law were men. In all public affairs—worship, politics, education, trade—it was a dominantly male society and it was altogether natural that traditional male symbols should have been used to describe God's relationship to his people. This conceptual framework was in no way repudiated by Jesus and his disciples. Yet it was in process of being vitally transformed by the new symbolism naming God as Father and Jesus as Son. It is probably in the experience of true fatherhood that the male shares most intensely in the expression of feminine qualities.

However the dispersion of early Christians out into the towns and villages of the Mediterranean world brought them into contact with a far more complex symbol-system; there were 'gods many and lords many'; there were temples and images; there was a bewildering variety of cults. Moreover the whole tradition was that of devotion to and dependence upon the land and the life of nature. Sacrifice, symbolically representing and promoting the death-life rhythm, was everywhere in evidence.

Yet as one reflects upon the political power of Rome and the extent of its military organization, it might seem at first sight that the Graeco-Roman world was dominantly patriarchal. But the tradition of 'the Mothers' was still immensely powerful. The principles of blood relationship, of affinities with nature, of cosmic wholeness were woven into the social fabric. Over the centuries the soil and the womb had been closely identified and agricultural labour had been viewed as comparable to the sexual act of generation. And although there were powerful male gods aplenty, it was the mysterious earth-mother that retained a tenacious hold upon the human imagination.

In a striking passage Professor W. K. C. Guthrie has commented on the general religious atmosphere of the Hellenistic world. Taking his cue from the writings of Hesiod he declares: 'A noteworthy feature of the whole account is the abiding influence of Gaia, the Earth, from the earliest generation to the latest, not as supreme ruler herself but as the universally acknowledged power behind the throne. Throughout the religious changes which took place in Greece, culminating in the vivid anthropomorphisms of the Olympian religion which the classical Greeks inherited from Homer, the awe inspired by the earth-mother never failed though she was recognized to be, as indeed she was, a far older power in the land than the Olympians. Nor were her prophetic powers forgotten. At Delphi itself she was acknowledged as the original tenant of the oracle, now presided over by Apollo on behalf of Zeus'. (*Cambridge Ancient History.* Revised Edition II.11.38)

It was into this atmosphere that Christian missionaries came with their gospel of the supreme God, Yahweh, who had sent his Son into the world to proclaim good news and to heal the sick and distressed and who, when the Son had been condemned to death on a cross, had raised him to newness of life. How could this gospel with its overwhelmingly male symbolism and its background of the history of a pilgrim people be related to a culture with an undergirding female symbolism and a background of settled life sustained continuously by the resources of soil and seed? Theologically, in the Jewish context, Jesus had taken the place of Torah (the Law); in the realm of popular religious feeling he had taken the place of Messiah, the conquering hero. In the Hellenistic world theologically he was to take the place of Logos (World-order); in the realm of popular religious feeling he would replace Apollo, son of Zeus, who had attained such eminence in Rome in the first century of our era. But whereas the overarching consciousness in the racial memory of the Jews was the victory of their God over all the forces of nature and the power of his word to order and direct the social life of his people, the parallel consciousness within the racial memory of dwellers in the Mediterranean world was that of the beneficence and fruitfulness of the earth-mother and of the wholeness of organic life in society which she had been able to generate and sustain.

IV

It was the daunting task of Christian missionaries, apologists, teachers, bishops to be faithful to this double heritage without allowing either to be submerged by the other. It is clear that the fall of Jerusalem in AD 70 virtually marked the end of any accommodations within Judaism such as had entered its religious life through contacts with its neighbours. Temple sacrifices ceased. Priesthood became simply nominal. Association with the land and its productivity became almost impossible. Survival depended on trade, crafts, education, while religion consisted in honouring the one God through prayers and obedience to his Law. It became increasingly a male-dominated culture with women confined to the care of home and family. From this cultural context Christianity was almost entirely excluded.

How then could it retain its Jewish heritage? Only by clinging to the Old Testament and to the Hebraic symbolisms of the New Testament, of its early sacramental observances and of its communal organization. The balance tipped heavily towards Hellenistic modes of interpretation, cult-practices and intellectual conceptualizations. Allegorization made possible the continued appeal to the Old Testament; sacrificial terminology came to be applied to the Lord's Supper and regenerative terminology to Baptism; Logos and Pneuma became key-terms for re-interpreting the concept of God. So far as male-female principles were concerned attention was focussed upon the mother-son relationship in the gospels and the performance of certain functions within the church by women was allowed. Celibacy and viginity as ideal forms of religious life were foreign to Hebrew culture but belonged naturally to the religious tradition of the Mediterranean world.

In retrospect it is hard to see how things could have been otherwise if Christianity was to survive within a context whose symbolic forms in art, literature and religion had developed primarily through relatedness to the natural order in its whole manner of life. There were indeed polarizing factors of high importance—the adventures of heroes, inter-tribal struggles and the establishment of formal law. But the basic framework of the economy remained intact and Catholic Christianity emerged as the purgation yet also as the fulfilment of this Hellenistic culture. The Father-Creator was confessed and worshipped but remained absolute in his transcendence. The Son occupied the central place as mediator and priests were ordained as his representatives. In varying ways the feminine and regenerative aspects of life were recognized symbolically; the Virgin and Child, the Mother of God, Mary the immaculate; the church as the spouse of Christ and mother of the faithful; the Spirit as Dove, as brooding over the waters, as fount of life and love (and at least in one region deaconesses were regarded as symbolic representatives of the Spirit).

Thus a symbolic framework came to receive general acceptance in which God as ruler was represented by the bishop; the Son as sacrificer and sacrifice by the priests; the Spirit by the church, regarded as bride and mother. There were challenges to this pattern from militant emperors, barons, knights and merchants but the religious symbolism held firm until the later Middle Ages. Then came the resurgence of the dynamic Hebrew symbolism of the Old Testament, interpreted now not allegorically and anagogically but realistically and historically.

Whatever may have been the diversified forces at work leading to the Reformation and the rise of modern science, one thing is clear. Within the new era it was man who rapidly grew in self-confidence as he invented new technological instruments and devised new forms of social organization. No longer was he held fast within a land-based economy and a divinely-sanctioned hierarchical society. He began to see himself as harnesser of wind and water, as controller of fire and as fashioner of iron and steel. Moreover he dared to conceive of human society in terms of voluntary associations of life-minded individuals. And the religious sanctions for these startling new possibilities he found in the Old Testament itself. The commission to have dominion over the earth, the prohibition of images and nature-worship, the sense of the divine control of all natural forces, inspired men to sail the seas, to exploit earth's treasures and to pry into the mysteries of the heavens. Further, the Old Testament witness to the centrality of the Covenant for social organization legitimized the formation of societies whose immediate aims were directed to betterment in this world but whose ultimate sanction, they believed, belonged to an eternal divine purpose.

Within all forms of Protestant, Reformed Christianity which made a radical break with the Roman tradition, any kind of *natural* symbolism was only sparingly used. Perhaps the commonest was that of the fire. The story of the bush that burned with fire held powerful implications. If man could learn the ways of God and could co-operate with him in the utilization of the energies released by fire, vast new transformations might be achieved. But more important were the new *social* possibilities. If men could enter afresh into covenant relationship with God and into loyal partnerships with one another, they could face with confidence a whole hierarchy of king and lords and their armies, even when supported by the power of the church. The new societies within this new religious framework gave an altogether new prominence to manly virtues and skills, appealing to the exploits of Old Testament heroes and leaders and re-discovering the New Testament imagery of Jesus as Victor and Deliverer. And so far as ministry was concerned, the all-important matter now was to set apart men who could rightly interpret the Scriptures as documents of command and destiny and could correctly perform the covenant ceremonies by which the Christian social order could be visibly sealed and confirmed. Woman's function, as in the ancient Hebrew context, was that of caring for home and family, while man was engaged in processes of adventure, conflict and exchange.

V

In spite of the growing influence upon European cultural life of commercial enterprises, geographical discoveries, scientific inventions and industrial developments the traditional emphases upon the land and its bounty, upon the rhythm of the seasons and the coming of the rain, upon fair distribution and continuing production were never completely eclipsed. The time had passed when an agrarian economy, sanctioned by an imposing religious symbolism, appeared to be impregnably established. The rise of science and industry, also sanctioned, at least at first, by an alternative religious symbolism had restored a polarity within Christianity such as had not existed since the early tension between Hebraic and Hellenistic patterns of life. But whereas feminine generative symbolism was still powerfully operative within the Catholic tradition, within Protestantism it was masculine symbolism which became publicly predominant. Science and its applications seemed to be a male preserve and a God who controlled the forces of the universe according to a system of mechanical laws seemed to provide the necessary sanction for man's experiments and constructions.

However a major revolution has come about in the past century in at least two ways. First have come radical questionings about the necessity for *any* religious sanction for human enterprises. Is not the universe self-contained, a vast mechanism which is neither male- nor female-oriented but simply the structuring of a neutral energy? Men and women find themselves in a universe the regularities of whose operations they can discover for themselves. It is up to them to do the best they can with those factors over which they can exercise some control. The even more important thing is for them to work out ways of living together without recourse to transcendent powers or divine sanctions. Male-female relationships depend entirely on what seems advantageous to society as a whole.

The second major change has come about through the advances of the life-sciences and the increasing reliance upon electrical energy. The hard sciences focussed attention upon the external world—sun, moon and stars, water, wind and fire, meals, tools, and fuel; the life sciences turned inwards to examine the body and its many parts, the processes of reproduction, health and disease, nutrition and genetics. Moreover whereas the hard sciences were originally concerned with the release of energy from external fuels, the life-sciences have directed attention increasingly to electrical forces operating within nature, within the human body, potentially within the atom itself. What has been called the second industrial revolution has come about through the harnessing of electrical energy in multitudinous ways and this form of power can be employed with virtually no expenditure of energy on the part of the human agent. Whereas in the first industrial revolution human strength and endurance were primary factors, now heavy processes are increasingly operated by machines while the manipulation of electrical machinery can be undertaken equally well by men or women.

But there has been another result of the progress of the life-sciences. Women's subjection to laborious travail in birth has been lightened, her release from an unlimited series of pregnancies has been made possible and the distinctive function of child-bearing, which was at once her glory and yet the handicap preventing her full participation in public life, has been radically transformed. The mysterious processes of conception and generation which seemed to be entirely beyond human control have now become not only open to regulation quantitatively but also, through the discovery of the genetic code, open to manipulation qualitatively. Woman can take part in public life as never before. At the same time the mystique of conception and birth, profoundly associated with patterns of religious symbolism, is being rapidly eroded. Can the conviction that sacrifice, life-through-death, exists as a principle at the very heart of reality, survive? Does the new emancipation hold out the prospect of a new and creative balance of male and female principles within the symbolic expression of Christianity in contrast to the largely opposed symbolic systems which have been in evidence from the sixteenth century almost to the present time?

VI

Finally, in the light of this rapid historical survey, I present a few reflections on the immediate question of the desirability of ordaining women to the ministerial priesthood. First it seems important to recall the fact that ordination is, in its primary meaning, an *ordering*, a putting in order. It is assumed that in any particular society there must be certain well-defined orders. Now in all societies order is established by the creation and subsequent public recognition of specific symbols. As Sir Raymond Firth has tersely said: 'Man does not live by symbols alone but man orders and interprets his reality by his symbols' (*Symbolism* p. 20). Space, time, social activities and relationships are represented symbolically and in this way order is created and preserved.

So important is order for the survival of a society and so highly valued consequently are the symbols by which its order is created that man has been constantly inclined to believe that a particular symbol-system is inviolable—that any deviation, through discard or even through re-arrangement, is a threat to that order on which his whole existence seems to depend. He fears chaos and meaninglessness. Once accepted, a symbolic framework seems to provide just the security that he needs.

Yet the very nature of a true symbol makes such a final security impossible. Two entities are brought together in a symbol but are not thereby completely fused and identified. If an absolute identification takes place symbolic relationship is terminated. Two-ness has disappeared. Inter-action and inter-animation are annulled and nothing more than a lifeless label or counter remains. Counters certainly have their use for dealing with lifeless objects but where person-to-person relationships are concerned possibilities of developments in knowledge and changes through creative actions must be allowed for. Above all symbols employed for the ordering of relationships *between man and God* must always remain open to amplification and re-interpretation and new creation.

Symbols are always human constructs fashioned in terms of relationships with the world and with fellow human beings. For Christians, the central and controlling symbol has been Jesus in his human career and in his death-resurrection. Of much of his human career we know nothing. But his teaching through parables, his ministry of healing, his relationships with his disciples and with the religious leaders of the time—these have been recorded in terms derived from the common human experiences of his time. Yet this particular human career so described is claimed to be the supreme symbol of the nature and activity of God himself. In and through it God and man have been brought together within a unique symbol whose implications are unlimited and whose applications to new situations are universal.

An essential part then of the vocation of every Christian has been that of the *imitatio Christi*, the re-interpretation within his or her own situation of the pattern of teaching, healing, approving, condemning, such as was manifested in the career of Jesus himself. And this pattern, constantly involving some form of self-giving, reaches a climax in the readiness to sacrifice even life itself. 'The good shepherd giveth his life for the sheep.... Greater love hath no man than this that a man lay down his life for his friends'. Through his followers in every age this symbolic pattern must in some way be expressed. The re-interpretation may be through the telling of imaginative story or through the performance of compassionate deed, through long endurance or through courageous action. In whatever way the central image of Jesus' own career is re-interpreted, the new symbol will point towards the pattern of life-through-death which he himself displayed. And when the pattern is highlighted through ritual drama, there can be no disqualification from playing particular roles save that of rejecting Jesus' own test of discipleship: 'Whosoever will save his life shall lose it; but whosoever will lose his life for my sake and the gospel's, the same shall save it.'

There is a second immensely powerful symbol at the heart of the Christian faith. It brings together an amazing conjunction of opposites—death and resurrection. Here is a togetherness which cannot be imitated; it can only be proclaimed. But how can it be proclaimed when nothing comparable has happened in human affairs or experience? This has ever been the dilemma of the Christian witness. The unique must be made known through *language* (in the widest sense of a symbol-system which includes both speech and action) and yet no language can be adequate.

The only possibility is that of grasping from human communications-systems conjunctions of names or of critical events which in some way point towards the bringing together of Jesus-in-his-death and the Son-of-God-in-resurrection life. From Jewish cultural history Son of Man—Son of God, Servant—Lord, Son of David—Messiah, The Humiliated—The Exalted. Or again the Exodus story of bondage and despair reversed by deliverance and hope, the shedding of blood conjoined with remission of sins. By the use of such symbolic forms early witnesses sought to proclaim the revolutionary news that God in his holiness and utter opposition to the pretensions and prejudices of mankind had yet broken through the seemingly impassable barrier and overcome all alienations through the critical reconciling act of Jesus' death-resurrection. 'God was in Christ reconciling the world to himself.' Henceforth it was an essential part of the vocation of every Christian, Jew or Gentile, male or female, to communicate, through symbols taken from their own particular cultures, the reconciliation of the apparently unreconcilable contraries—the righteous God and alienated humankind. And for this task there can be no disqualification save that of rejecting the belief that such an act of reconciliation has indeed been effected or refusing to seek language-forms to bring together the reconciling act and the culture in which his or her own life is set.

How far then can woman today represent the Christ who throughout the centuries has been envisaged as primarily a masculine figure? Physically she obviously cannot do so. Psychologically she can to a greater degree than was at one time imagined if it is true that male and female attitudes and qualities are possessed in varying combinations by every human being. Symbolically—and it is by using symbols that man and woman transcend the physical and literal—in the context where Christ stands before us as *Generator and Sustainer and Fulfiller of Life* ('I am come that they might have life and that they might have it more abundantly') and as *Reconciler of Opposites into unhindered Communication* ('You that were sometime alienated and enemies hath he reconciled: through him we have access by one Spirit to the Father') can she not be admitted to the ordering of those who are thereby privileged, according to time and circumstance, to represent the Christ in the sustaining of the life of the Body and in the communicating of the word of reconciliation to the world?

CHAPTER 4

VOCATIONAL AND PASTORAL ASPECTS

MARY MICHAEL SIMPSON

Some Personal Reflections

The Episcopal Church was a joy and wonder to me when I discovered it as a senior in college and was confirmed. Upon graduation, I said, 'If I had been a man, I would have gone to seminary and become a priest.' At that point, in the mid-1940s, I did not question the system. It was obvious to me that I was not a man, and therefore could not become a priest. I did not even ask 'Why can't I?'

I wanted to study theology, and not only the priesthood, but even episcopal seminaries were closed to women. I talked with my bishop, who had me confer with a deaconess who worked in the diocese, and I soon found myself on the way to the New York Training School for Deaconesses and Other Church Workers, where I spent the next two years.

Of those who were in school with me at that time, none became deaconesses. Some of us joined religious orders, some married clergy, some found being an 'Other Church Worker' so unsatisfactory they went into secular occupations. So far as I know, I am the only one of the group who has finally been ordained to the priesthood, and I am wondering how many priestly vocations were thus lost.

I spent three years as a professional church worker—first as the assistant to a college chaplain, and then as a foreign missionary. It was from the depths of the African bush that I felt God was calling me to be a nun. When my tour ended, I went back home and entered the Order of St Helena as a postulant.

The religious life, as it then was, approached priesthood as closely as was possible for women at that time. Theologically educated women have complained, and justifiably so, that any snippet of a girl could put on a habit and get more recognition and respect than a lay woman could earn with all her degrees and accomplishments.

Although ours was a non-sacramental ministry, and thus 'lay' as compared with ordained, sisters were recognizably professional in the church, and thus were not 'lay' in another sense. We spoke in parishes at the principal services, carefully avoiding the pulpit. We gave 'addresses' rather than 'sermons' and joked about being haunted by St Paul for speaking in the church. The religious habit made us seen as official representatives of the church, so that on trains and planes we often heard confessions, though were denied the power to give absolution.

In the late 1960s, I found myself Novice Director and Vocations Director of the Order of St Helena. Among aspirants to the Order were young women who also felt that they had a vocation to the priesthood. To be able to relate to them and help them in their vocational quest, I began trying to work through from a biblical and theological standpoint the whole question of women's ordination. My reading and thinking led me to the conclusion that there was no barrier to the ordination of women; it just had not been done. I experienced a bittersweet response to this conclusion, composed of joy that it would soon be possible, and regret that it had not come a quarter of a century sooner, in time for me.

Having decided that ordination was acceptable for women in general, I had yet to decide whether or not it was for me. I was in my forties, settled into my vocation as a Religious for twenty years. On the other hand, the Holy Spirit seemed to be inspiring second vocations in many quarters and the results were creative and exciting. I could probably count on at least twenty years in which to exercise a priestly ministry. By the summer of 1973,

I had decided that God was indeed calling me to the priesthood, and had probably been doing so for many years. And once I believed that, I could make but one response: I decided to go ahead.

The Order of St Helena had set up a procedure by which life professed sisters could apply for permission to seek ordination to the diaconate, so I obtained that permission and began the process of seeking ordination through regular diocesan channels just before the General Convention met in Louisville, Kentucky in the Fall of 1973. I went to that General Convention convinced of my vocation to the priesthood and assuming that the church would validate what 'seemed good to the Holy Spirit and to me'. It did not.

Only after the failure in the House of Deputies in Louisville did I begin actively working for the ordination of women. I began serving on committees and panels, taking speaking engagements on the subject, along with my continuing progress towards ordination to the diaconate. And opportunities were plentiful ... National Task Force on Women, Diocesan Committee on the Ordination of Women, Episcopal Women's Caucus, etc.

About three months after the Louisville General Convention I attended a national meeting of women who were aspiring to priesthood, and it was a revelation to me. It was my first experience of being in a group of women who had been working for ten years or more to fulfill their vocation, and were very tired; and others who, like me, were more recently on the scene and enthusiastic and ready to engage in the struggle. At that meeting the mantle of responsibility passed from the one to the other —from those who had borne the burden and heat of the day to others who were latecomers into the vineyard. One of the joys of relating to these women has been involvement in a group where there was growing respect and love for one another under one overriding goal, but many different ways of approaching it.

July 29, 1974 was a watershed in the movement for the acceptance of women priests. On that day in Philadelphia, Pa., four bishops ordained eleven women to the priesthood, amid much joy, anguish, and controversy. I was not present. Being only a candidate for Holy Orders, I could not be invited to be ordained. As I was scheduled for surgery that day, I was spared making the decision whether or not to attend. But had it been otherwise, I suspect I would have stayed away. It seemed to me that what was happening was a grave mistake—disobedience, which could only cause us all trouble. Speculation of 'what if' is fruitless, but I now see what happened quite differently. I believe it was obedience to conscience informed by the Holy Spirit, that the opposition to women's ordination was so deep that all approaches were necessary, and that without it I would probably still be a deacon hoping for ordination to the priesthood. I owe my debt to the courageous women and bishops who took part in that ordination.

I was ordained to the diaconate by the Rt Rev. J. Stuart Wetmore, Suffragan Bishop of New York, in December, 1974, and was amazed at the impact it had on me. I had been in the 'inner circles' of the church so long that I had no starry-eyed idealism about the clergy, and yet here, as at my Life Profession and later at my ordination to the priesthood, there was a tremendous uplift, a sense of rightness between me and God and his world.

Immediately after ordination, I joined the staff of the Cathedral Church of St John the Divine, where I have a liturgical and pastoral ministry. I was at that time a student in pastoral counselling. I had realized earlier that people were coming to me with problems for which I was not prepared; I needed more skills. I studied for four years at the Westchester Institute for Training in Counseling and Psychotherapy, from which I graduated in June, 1976, just seven months before ordination to the priesthood.

We all approached the 1976 General Convention with apprehension—those of us who wanted women to be ordained were afraid it would fail again, and those who did not want it were afraid it would pass. I joined a group called 'Talk-it-out: Check-it-out' sponsored jointly by the Episcopal Women's Caucus and the Committee for the Apostolic Ministry—a conservative group which opposed women's ordination, but said they would not leave the church no matter what happened. The purpose of this operation was to squelch rumours and allow people to talk about how they felt about what was going on. It also served the purpose of allowing those who disagreed on so much to work together for the common good.

On the day of the fateful vote in the House of Deputies, after all the debate, Dr John Coburn, President of the House, called for a time of silence, and asked that there be no public display when the vote was announced. The silence was intense, and after the announcement of the decision, was broken only by an occasional sob or sigh. The Archbishop of Canterbury was there, and with this decision made, urged us on to the bringing in of the kingdom.

It was a difficult time in some ways, because in spite of our joy we were conscious of those who were suffering. The priest who had presented me for confirmation was one of the speakers against women's ordination at the Convention. Some of my own Sisters were opposed, though once the church approved, none of them would have tried to prevent me from fulfilling my vocation. In fact, three members of the Order are now priests. It seems to me that we were giving more compassion than we had received three years before, but perhaps that was because we knew what it felt like, and were more able to empathize.

Once back home, the Diocesan Bishop of New York, the Rt Rev. Paul Moore, Jr met with the women deacons of his diocese to plan for the long-awaited ordinations which could be set for January, 1977. He found that each of us wanted to be ordained where we were ministering instead of in one great and glorious ceremony. So he began working many ordinations in the bishops' schedules instead of just one. January was a busy month, with each of us trying to get to as many ordinations as possible of those to whom we had become close in recent years.

I was ordained priest on January 9, 1977, thirty-one years after making the statement with which I opened this paper. This was the first time Bishop Moore had ordained a woman, and he had put so much of himself into making this possible, as he had with other causes in which he believed over the years, that he was obviously moved. He spoke of the fact that this was the first nun in the history of the whole church to be ordained to the priesthood, and what that meant in terms of bringing different strands of history together. He also recognized Carter Heyward as priest of the diocese in good standing, and spoke of all they had been through together before and after the Philadelphia ordination.

Next morning celebrating the eucharist for the first time, I thought of St Augustine's phrase 'ever ancient and ever new'. The same words, the same action I had experienced with other celebrants day after day over the years was suddenly gloriously new. A friend who had never before participated in a eucharist with a woman celebrant said 'Well, it was the Mass—and what was all the fuss about?' That is a reaction I have heard in other words, many times since.

I have gone on celebrating the eucharist at the cathedral on a regular basis, and at other places when I have been invited. I consider this one of the most important aspects of my ministry, and not only because of the centrality of the eucharist to the faith. I believe the time for talking about women's ordination has passed, that people will be converted by our Lord himself as they receive him in the eucharist at the hands of a woman, and it is important to provide an opportunity for that conversion.

To bring my own vocational story up to date, I was installed on October 9, 1977 as Canon Residentiary of the Cathedral of St John the Divine, with the title 'Canon Counsellor' and the responsibility for all the counselling services offered by the Cathedral. I had the feeling at that time that all the different strands of my life were converging—the theological and the spiritual and the psychological—to make it possible for me to do the work which God has prepared for me to walk in.

What it Feels Like

Next to the question 'What do you call a woman priest?' I am most often asked 'What does it feel like to be a woman and a priest?' This is asked by men who are priests, by women who are not, and by laymen who are neither. At first glance that seems to be a question which is analysable into two: What is it like to be a woman? and What is it like to be a priest? But there is a third which is implied, and which is often what is really meant: What does it feel like to be in such a controversial position?

Volumes have been written through the women's movement about what it means in today's world to be a woman who knows herself to be a person, made in God's image, and yet facing prejudices and discrimination which become more and more intolerable to her as her consciousness is raised. Unfortunately, the church is not free from the attitudes which taint our society in this regard. So this is one element of what it feels like.

For example, the American House of Bishops meeting in Florida recently issued a pastoral letter containing a so-called 'Conscience Clause' which stated that no bishop would be forced to ordain a woman, and nobody would be in jeopardy for refusing to recognize the ministry of ordained women. While freedom of conscience is a right, and the statement really contains nothing new, many of us are keenly aware that the House of Bishops has not felt it appropriate to issue such a statement in regard to other groups—Male priests, Black priests, Hispanic priests, Oriental priests, or Gay priests.

Becoming a priest is indescribably wonderful. Perhaps it is particularly true of a long-delayed vocation that there is a sense of 'coming home', of 'this is where I should be', of having found my seat in life. Since it is a spiritual home, it brings with it a security that comes with having one's treasures where 'neither moth nor rust doth corrupt and where thieves cannot break through and steal'. God's grace and bounty is suddenly showered forth, and I had a sense that never before had I known such joy and fulfilment. Though it is difficult to communicate feelings of this sort, I would assume that something like this is more or less universal in regard to being ordained priest, and not just true of women.

I have tried to separate the two questions above, but neither I nor anybody else can possibly know what it will be like to be a priest who happens also to be a woman once all the furore has died down. Indeed, some of it has died down now. I am in one sense 'second generation'. My life as a priest is different, much calmer, than that of the women who were ordained in Philadelphia in 1974. But now, in the first year of officially recognized ordinations of women, it still means living very much as a symbol. That opens one to all the projections of people's feelings about women, about authority, about motherhood, about sexuality, and a whole list of other things. There are people who love me and people who hate me without ever seeing me.

For example, on the day I am writing this, one of the letters which arrived in the morning mail was from an unknown priest in a distant part of the country. It read, in part: 'Sister, please don't delude yourself that you have been ordained into the One Holy Catholic and Apostolic Church. The 1976 General Convention is a Pan Protestant body which is just one in a long series of steps catering to the whims of heretical priests and bishops. But God will have His day! Maranatha.' The same mail brought a carbon of a letter to the editor of a national church magazine referring to me as 'abusive and abrasive' for my statement that it is those who gathered in St Louis to form a new church who bear the responsibility for schism, rather than the ordained women. And there are letters which are just as unrealistic on the positive side.

Now, I believe none of this, and am not unduly worried by it. But woe betide the person who internalizes all this and identifies with her role. In the above cases, she would doubt the validity of her ordination, as well as her intention to be courteous to those with whom she differs. In general, such a person would be in continual flux from the heights to the depths of depression. So it is necessary, while accepting that one is a 'priest forever after the order of Melchizedek' to separate oneself out and maintain enough distance not to personalize people's reactions to the ordination of women.

Impact on those to whom I minister

In my understanding of theology, since priesthood is a supernatural gift from God, it is not dependent on the gender of the person being ordained, any more than it is on the personality, education, mental health or any other quality. The people I baptize, marry, communicate or absolve, receive exactly the same sacraments as though they had been baptized, married, communicated, or absolved by any other human being who has been ordained, and in that sense, it really doesn't matter.

This supernatural view of ordination has, of course, tremendous implications for the church in its decision-making process about whether or not to ordain women. If we were a social club, we would have a right to decide whom we would authorize to function for us. On the other hand, if ordination is God's gift of which he had made his church the repository, we bestow it on whomever he has called, and withhold it from such at our peril.

I believe that because we as women have had a different experience from men, priests who are women have a special contribution to make to the well-being of women and children. And not only to them. Each human being has a feminine as well as a masculine nature. Along a vast spectrum, some of us have more femininity and some more masculinity. Priests who are women can speak to that feminine nature in a way that is different from others priests.

Because of our past experience, some of us relate better to women and some to men. Thus, there is a positive as well as a negative aspect to what I was saying in the previous section about the tendency to project onto priests who are women all our feelings from the past about women, authority, etc. As one priest said after he had come to me to make his confession: 'Once you get over the hang-up about telling your mother of your sexual misdeeds, it can be very helpful.'

The congregation at the midweek eucharist at the cathedral at which I am the celebrant is growing. It is composed not only of radicals, or only of women, but of people to whom it is important, and I believe some of them are at that particular celebration because I am a woman. When I am away, they come up after my return and say they missed me and ask where I was last week. And many people—men as well as women—say that though they themselves don't want to be ordained, it means so much to them to have me at the altar. 'It means that the church really accepts me—I'm not a second-class citizen.'

In ministering as a priest, as in any of the so-called helping professions, my primary tool is myself. From that point of view, every aspect of who I am is important —that I have a certain personality, education, experience, certain interests and abilities—and that I am a woman.

A whole priesthood

One of the organizations working for the ordination of women at the General Convention in Minneapolis in 1976 had a button which read 'Celebrate a Whole Priesthood'. And I believe that is the issue. The church has coped for almost 2,000 years with a priesthood the candidates for which were selected from only one half of the human race. The church, and the world, were not ready. Perhaps this is one of the multitude of things our Lord meant when he said 'I have many things to tell you, but you cannot bear them now'. It makes one wonder what is yet to be told.

A book which appeared some years ago by Caryll Houselander was entitled *The Reed of God*. It compared Mary, the Mother of Jesus, to a hollow reed of the sort children use for making whistles. God the Holy Spirit could blow through her as he would. She was the instrument of communication between God and his world. The same phrase, I think, could be applied to priests. As representatives of his church, we are to be instruments of communication between God and the rest of humanity. We are to be symbols of the Holy. This is a tremendous and awesome responsibility—the realization that people judge not only the church but God himself by what his priests are.

From the time of the patriarchs of the Old Testament right up till the present the symbolism has been male, though we know intellectually that since all that is good is contained within God, it is impossible for God to be male any more than female, and insofar as one is contained within the Godhead, so is the other. It is all very well to say that the masculine term is generic and includes the feminine, but it is true that the way we talk affects the way we think.

The qualities we associate with masculinity are power, wisdom, justice, etc. In spite of the fact that these qualities are balanced by their opposites in the scholarly theological tomes, the popular image of God has remained the old man with a long white beard sitting on a throne in heaven. When the symbolism for God is totally male, many begin to think of the stern judge who is just but lacking in sympathy, distant, and even cruel. Understanding of the meaning of 'Father' will depend to some extent on one's own experience, but the hunger for the feminine, for 'Mother', remains. There are a number of ways of meeting this hunger, of attempting to correct the distortion in understanding which is created by a one-sided symbolism. The one found in the Middle Ages was to exalt Mary to the position of Mediatrix, to soften the dealings of God with us and plead our cause.

Even today there are many who speak of 'Holy Mother Church'. Granted that this may be partially accounted for by a neurotic desire to see ourselves as children and be taken care of, it may also be a genuine sign of our need for the feminine in our symbolism. And of course, the other is the current demand for a whole priesthood—one composed of women as well as of men. There are no role-models for the women who have come into the priesthood, so it is a wonderous and awesome thing to feel one's way along strange paths, and an equally wondrous thing to realize that for the generations of young women yet to grow up, we will be the role-models, that a new option will be added for them, now that we have a whole priesthood.

I feel especially blessed in my present position in having a part in acting out this symbol of the whole priesthood. It is less possible where one is working in isolation, but where a group of clergy work together as a team, all different aspects of humanity can be represented. I am the only woman priest on the staff of the cathedral, but my brother priests represent a variety which is a microcosm of the Body of Christ. Among us there are Black and Hispanic priests as well as Caucasian. And the different forms of expertise contained within the Chapter make it possible for us to have a 'whole' priesthood with which to minister to those who come to the cathedral.

Ministering to the whole person

The compartmentalization of life today is notorious, with the field of expertise any one person can have ever narrowing. For social and biological reasons most women have developed a holistic and practical attitude towards life as opposed to one that is specialized and abstract. Running a home and raising a family demands that one be to some extent a jack of all trades, and social pressures have kept the most lucrative fields of specialization closed to women until recently.

Through the ages in the pain of childbirth, through dealing with personal problems which arise at every stage in the lives of loved ones, and finally through the care of the sick and dying, women have had an opportunity to centre in on all that is individual and deeply human. This human dimension is one that is sorely needed in our technological age of computerized decisions and mass organization.

My own ministry is currently pointing in this direction. With the help of a group of specialists in the fields of psychiatry, psychology, social work, pastoral counselling, and psychiatric nursing, I am trying to establish at the Cathedral of St John the Divine a Pastoral Counselling Centre. This will deal with the person individually and in groups in the situation in which he finds himself in today's world with all his existential problems—his loneliness, alienation, and confusion about his identity and future path. It will provide him with a Christian ministry of healing, some Christian answers and light along the path. The 'cure of souls' is the church's business; perhaps we can help restore it to the central place it once had. The church can do this in a way that cannot be done by those lacking in Christian motivation. And women can add a dimension to this effort.

CHAPTER 5

AN EPISCOPAL ACCOUNT OF WOMEN PRIESTS

GILBERT BAKER

The parish church with the Chinese roof stands near the airport. Amid the noise of traffic and descending planes Sunday service is about to begin. The large choir, of men and women, stands outside, ready for prayer, with surplices fluttering in the wind. At the end of the procession in clerical robes is the Reverend Jane Hwang. At first sight she looks like an average and kindly Sunday School teacher, and she has a deceptively mild manner. But once she takes a lead in the service, whether she is preaching, or celebrating the eucharist, there is no mistaking the genuine devotion and the quiet note of authority of the priest.

The church is full. There is a large number of young people, and it is significant that a number of them—more than in any other of our parishes—have become candidates for ordination, through the influence of their vicar. There are many families in church too, and a number of elderly and mostly poor women.

After the service there is a gathering for tea in the parish house. If I am there and a confirmation has taken place, the newly confirmed, usually about forty to fifty, are introduced, and each one is presented with a devotional book.

Later, Jane goes to the home of a sick church member to bring him the sacrament; or she may go on to the ecumenical Old People's Home and celebrate Holy Communion for the Anglican members there.

For the first few years that Jane was vicar she was also principal of a church primary school in a tough new housing estate up against the Kowloon hills. While she was there she organized a Sunday School for the children, and this has since grown to be one of our new congregations, the Kindly Light Church.

At our weekly meetings for clergy, which follow Holy Communion and breakfast, I find that when discussion sometimes descends to the trivial it is usually Jane who brings us back to a spiritual plane. She commands the respect of all our clergy by the sheer quality of spiritual life and her record of action.

Joyce Bennett, with Jane, had been in deacon's orders for about ten years at the time of their ordination to the priesthood in 1971. We did not have to look around for candidates; for these two had held responsible positions in the diocese for many years.

Joyce is English, a missionary of the CMS—a teacher who has worked at both school and university level; she is now Principal of St Catharine's Secondary School for Girls in the industrial suburb of Kwuntong. She has been very active on our diocesan committees for Primary Schools and Religious Education; and it is significant that several years after her ordination, because of her widespread experience of education and knowledge of the social conditions of girls in her school and their families, she was invited in 1976 by the Governor of Hong Kong to serve on the Legislative Council.

This gives her a remarkable opportunity for asserting Christian influence in public affairs, and I believe that all this stems from her experience as an ordained priest.

For in addition to her leadership of a first-class school Joyce has shown a deep pastoral concern for the girls and the families from which they come.

A girl does badly in class or wants to drop out. It is discovered that there is a family problem. Parents press their children to stay at home or work in a factory. Sometimes truancy leads along the brightly lit but dangerous road to sleazy bars and drugs. But St Catharine's girls know that whatever happens they have a headmistress who cares.

Speaking to a Rotary Club about this pastoral side of her work Joyce said:

'None of this is possible without fulfilling the truly sacramental function of the priest—the celebration of the Holy Communion. In this service the priest is the instrument for the divine to come into the material world in a very special way. How often do we rail against this material society of Hong Kong in which we work? I believe that as a priest I am able in the sacrament to let God be made known in the world of men. Therefore once a week in school, after a mid-day meal we break the bread and pour out the wine to show forth again our Lord's death and proclaim what this means in our so-called secular world in the twentieth century.'

There is no doubt about the Christian character and very pleasant atmosphere of St Catharine's, even though of course the majority of girls are non-Christian.

On Sundays Joyce is usually at nearby St Barnabas' Church where she assists the Chinese priest and often preaches in her fluent Cantonese. Her ability in the language makes her very much a part of the whole life of the diocese; and as she has been here since 1949 she has a very wide range of friends who do not feel that there is anything very strange in her ministry.

Pauline Shek who was ordained priest in 1973 is chaplain at St Catharine's and on Sundays assists at Kei Oi (Christ's Love) Church in North Kowloon. She is quiet but has a remarkable way of getting on to the wave length of young people. She produces Christian drama, is interested in symbolism and art forms, and seems to understand the depths of young people's solitude and frustration—as well as knowing how to relate this to the saving hope which we all have in Christ.

It was perhaps characteristic that at a great Diocesan Youth Conference in the summer of 1977 when over 900 young people gathered from our parishes and schools Pauline was chosen to give the opening address to the crowds as they assembled in the open air. Her subject was 'Who am I?'

Mary Au is the only one of our four women priests who

has gone right through the preparation for the ministry in my time as bishop. She had been at Bishop Hall Jubilee Secondary School and was an enthusiastic member of Calvary Church. She had the intense experience of wanting to give her life to Christ, and I persuaded her to go to the Theological Division of Chung Chi College, now part of the Chinese University of Hong Kong. At first it seemed a daunting experience for Mary did not find study easy. But she very quickly became an outstanding leader in college affairs, and I kept hearing about her joyful and positive influence abong students and faculty alike.

She served her diaconate under Jane Hwang at Holy Trinity, and then became part time chaplain at her old school. Here she teaches religious knowledge, takes care of the Christian fellowship, organizes baptism classes and celebrates Holy Communion in the school chapel dedicated in the name of Bishop Alopen, the Nestorian leader of the first Christian mission who in AD 635 came from Persia to China.

But in Hong Kong a great many people including the clergy do more than one job; so Mary Au found herself in charge of the new congregation which Jane Hwang has started. It is called 'Kindly Light' Church for it is in a district called Tsz Wan Shan which could be translated 'Kindly (merciful) Cloud Mountain'. The church which meets in the primary school has grown considerably in the last few years. There is an able band of young men and women who serve as the church council. A flat has been purchased in the neighbourhood, and is the centre of parish activity, young people's groups, and for prayer and Bible study.

After Jane Hwang's initiative the work of organizing the congregation fell to the Rev. Louis Tsui who as a priest and a teacher in the school gathered a team of members who were really keen to take responsibility. When he left for further study in England the Reverend Mary Au was appointed. There seemed to be no basic difficulty about her following a male priest.

Naturally there is a difference in style as there always is

between one vicar and the next. But throughout these years—apart from a few anonymous letters at the time of Jane Hwang's ordination—I have had no complaints formal or otherwise about any of these four women—on the contrary the reports are generally very good.

They are all very different, and they do different kinds of jobs. There are some parishes where they might not fit in so well, and I know that some of the clergy who were not happy about the decision on ordination may still have reservations. But as one of our senior clergy said to me: 'I made my views known, but once the Synod made its decision then I accepted it completely.'

It so happens that none of the four women priests in this diocese is married. In each case this is a personal decision and is in no way a condition of ordination. I think that there might be some difficulties for a married woman priest, but they could be overcome. One of our women theological students who was easily the most brilliant in the Department of Theology in the Chinese University of Hong Kong has married and is teaching and serving as a lay chaplain in one of our schools. But she would certainly be eligible for ordination just as a man would be.

For some women, as for some men, celibacy in the priesthood is a vocation; but I do not think this is for all. Indeed in the pastoral counselling to young people the counselling of a young married woman, like that of a young married man could well be more effective than that of a celibate priest, male or female.

But so much depends on the individual in all these matters. I am sure that a bishop must be guided in his task of making choice of fit persons to serve in the sacred ministry of the church, not by a blanket rule which would debar some and admit others, but by a consideration, after prayer and the best advice he can get, whether or not he or she would be a faithful and effective priest.

Clearly there are some women who should not be ordained, just as there certainly are men who should not, and it is always the difficult task of a bishop or his advisers to show some people that an inner sense of call is not by itself a guarantee of ordination. This is an obvious point, but I make it because some bishops who have ordained women have been suspected of wildly and suddenly laying hands on all kinds of people.

In our diocese everyone who is ordained to the priesthood must present a resolution from his or her parish as well as satisfying the examining chaplains, and the name is then presented to the Standing Committee of the Diocesan Synod. The bishop has the final decision, but it is not without the support and endorsement of the diocese.

In each of the ordinations in which women have been ordained I have also ordained men at the same service. This avoids any suggestion of staging an ordination to prove some point; and for me the laying of hands on men and women at the same service symbolizes the unity of the priesthood and mutual acceptance in the ministry.

I am sometimes asked what special gifts women bring to the total ministry of the church. Everyone has peculiar gifts—of prayer, or personal relationship, scholarship, or a capacity to take a lead in parish and social affairs. I would say that women carry out their priestly ministry in a distinctive style. Generally I find that our women priests have a directness and a courage in facing difficulties, perhaps a quietness and simplicity of faith. They are not too self-conscious about their position. They do not wear clerical dress in schools or on their parish rounds; but they are always correctly robed in church.

For the quiet steady work of evangelism, visiting church members, especially the old and the very young, the ministry of women is invaluable; and there is room for more ordained women to care for girls in factories, in schools and colleges, and in rescue work for those in need of care.

But the gift which women bring to the priesthood may be seen theologically as a step towards the fulfilment of Christ's intention. For the priesthood is not ours to confer or withhold, it is Christ's. As the Proper Man, the representative of humanity, he is the High Priest for us all, men and women alike. Therefore it seems that men and women should partake in the priesthood of Christ.

The question is often asked: 'Why was Hong Kong the first diocese to ordain women to the priesthood?' The story goes back more than thirty years to wartime China. Florence Lee Tim Oi, a graduate of Union Theological College, Canton, had been ordained in deacon's orders in 1941. She was appointed to the congregation in Macao, the Portuguese colony forty miles west of Hong Kong. After the Japanese occupation of Hong Kong and much of South China it was impossible for a Chinese priest to get to Macao to celebrate Holy Communion. As a wartime measure the Assistant Bishop Mok Sau Tseng, in the absence of my predecessor Bishop R. O. Hall, gave Florence Lee permission to celebrate. Bishop Hall, on his return from America and Britain, decided to ordain her; she made her way to the mainland, and was made priest on St Paul's Day 1944 in Shiuhing.

After the war Bishop Hall explained his action to the Diocesan Synod which unanimously supported his action. A draft canon to allow an experimental period for women's ordination was taken to the General Synod of the Chung Hua Sheng Kung Hui (Holy Catholic Church of China) in 1947, but this was rejected. Instead a question was put to the Lambeth Conference of 1948 asking if one church in the Anglican Communion could be free to ordain women on such an experimental basis, this would be in accordance with Anglican tradition. The Lambeth Fathers said it would not. Meanwhile Florence Lee, to save Bishop Hall and the church from embarrassment, had resigned her priest's orders and remained a deacon; she continued to serve in South China until the cultural revolution of 1966.

Thus the diocese felt it had already accepted women's ordination in principle when the matter came up again after the Lambeth Conference of 1968. I attended as a rather new bishop and found that the climate of opinion had changed considerably. The present Archbishop of Canterbury had chaired a commission whose report made no secret of its expectation that ordination of women to the priesthood would probably come.

The resolutions of the Lambeth Conference on this

subject (thirty-four to thirty-eight) request every national and regional church or province to give careful study to the question and recommended that 'before any national or regional church makes a final decision to ordain women to the priesthood the advice of the Anglican Consultative Council should be sought and carefully considered'.

These resolutions were reported to the Council of the Church of South-East Asia which met in Taiwan in April 1969. In the summer I set up a small working party to consider next steps; the members reported that they could see no reason against women's ordination and suggested that Hong Kong would be a suitable place in which initiative could be taken. Before much could be done we had three resolutions before Diocesan Synod advocating the ordination of women.

When the Diocesan Synod met in November 1969 we realized there had not been enough time for study. We therefore postponed this question, and called another Synod in January. In the meantime I sent out a paper to the parishes, outlining as far as possible the pros and cons on the whole subject. Every parish vestry or council was asked to meet and give a reply in two months. I think there was a serious effort to grapple with the question in most of our parish meetings. When the returns came they showed that only one rather small parish positively objected to the ordination of women to the priesthood.

These results were made known when the Synod reconvened in January 1970. After a considerable debate the voting on the question was sixty-seven in favour, eight against and seventeen abstained.

When Synod asked me what I proposed to do I replied that I could not act unilaterally, and I would have first to consult my brother bishops. I did so at a meeting in Kuching, Borneo in February 1970. We felt that as a regional group of bishops the question of women's ordination was not one on which we could decide. But the Anglican Advisory Council had been set up and we agreed to refer Hong Kong's question to this body.

A year went by. I did not try to exercise influence or

pressure, because I think the Holy Spirit is surely guiding the church in this as in other matters. I was inclined to take a Gamaliel-like, perhaps a pragmatic view of new developments. If this thing was of God then it would become clear in the fruits of women's ministry. If it were not, then presumably the church would be shown with unmistakable clarity that it should not proceed any further.

When the Anglican Consultative Council met in Limuru, Kenya in 1971 there was a spirited debate on the question presented by the Diocese of Hong Kong. The advice given by a small majority was that if the Bishop of Hong Kong proceeded to ordain women to the priesthood such an action would be acceptable to the Council, and that all the Provinces and regional Councils of the Anglican Communion would be encouraged to remain in communion with the diocese.

The Council of the Church of South-East Asia which met in Hong Kong in April 1971 did not support us, but did not oppose us either. It merely 'witheld advice' which was not exactly helpful, but I could see why our neighbouring dioceses took that line. For none of them were really free to make a decision. Taiwan and the Philippine Episcopal Church had to wait for the Episcopal Church of USA, and the other Anglican dioceses came under the jurisdiction of Canterbury.

As a diocese Hong Kong and Macao is constitutionally part of the Chung Hua Sheng Kung Hui, and the Council of the Church of South-East Asia is the custodian of the Constitution. However one interpreted the Canons (and I personally believe they do not require changing for in the statements about priesthood there is no mention of the sex of the person to be ordained) we are in a position where the existing Canons and Constitution are virtually unalterable.

So I was left to decide alone. I remember my colleagues saying 'What are you going to do now?' And I knew that as in so many other happenings in a bishop's life the decision comes back, and as the saying is 'the buck stops here'. There were those whose judgement I deeply respected who advised delay. Others no less weighty in their wisdom and experience felt that to ignore the advice of the Anglican Consultative Council would be to question its authority, and also miss a great opportunity to make an act of faith on behalf of the whole church. I prayed and thought about it all that summer, and in the end I came to the conclusion that before God I could not in conscience refuse to ordain the two women whose names had come before me while at the same time proceeding with the ordination of two equally suitable and much younger men.

Our Diocesan Synod met in November 1971. I announced in my charge that I intended to proceed with the ordinations at Advent and set out the events which had occurred since the last meeting. We had already passed the motion in favour of ordaining women to the priesthood; someone wanted to re-open the question, but this proved not to be the wish of the Synod.

So Jane Hwang and Joyce Bennett were ordained on Advent Sunday, 28 November 1971 together with the two men, and Pauline Shek was ordained deacon. St John's Cathedral was full to overflowing. Some of course came for the news-value but there was also a tremendous and positive response from the diocese. For as many of the older people recalled, the diocese had made its decision in 1945 in response to Bishop Hall's action, and they saw no reason to change their minds.

Naturally there were a good many letters, mostly favourable, a number were critical or sorrowful; a few were almost abusive. No bishop or province or national church said anything about not remaining in communion with our diocese.

Since the ordination we have had visits from the then Archbishop of Canterbury (Dr Ramsey), two successive Presiding Bishops of the Episcopal Church USA, the Primates of Canada, Australia, New Zealand, All Ireland and other bishops from many parts of the world. I have also been graciously welcomed in a number of churches of the Anglican Communion in four continents in the last few years.

I do not think that our relations with the Roman Catholic Church in this diocese have been altered in any way since the ordinations. I wrote to my friend the late Bishop Hsu about my intention to ordain. He was away at the time, but he wrote a very sympathetic and understanding letter. It was after this that we worked very closely together on educational matters. Many Roman Catholics, including Jesuit fathers and a number of sisters said how thankful they were that we had taken this step. Joyce Bennett has been asked to preach at Mass and to speak of her experience as a priest to sisters of two religious orders.

We have in the last few years made an agreement with the Roman Catholic diocese about baptism and are now engaged in conversations about Christian marriage. The fact that we have women priests has not broken relations—they have in fact grown deeper and closer in recent years. As for relations in the other direction I have not found that even those who believe most strongly that the Bible gives detailed directions for church government have made any protest. One of the largest churches, the Church of Christ in China (Presbyterian and Congregational) have had women in their ministry for many years.

The presence of women in the ministry has, I believe, generally had a wholesome effect in the diocese. Of course there must be moments when an ordained man will complain 'How like a woman!' and doubtless their sisters in Christ have occasion to murmur 'How like a man!' For we are not pretending to have a uni-sex ministry; if it is truly incarnational our priesthood is fully human, and people will find a wholeness in life when the grace of God is communicated through the pastoral work of men and women.

After standing for four years alone we are thankful to have been joined by the Anglican Church of Canada, the Episcopal Church of USA and the Church of the Province of New Zealand. Other churches of the Anglican communion, including the Church of England, have agreed that there are no theological objections to the course we have pursued.

I have not been very keen on the militancy of some of the women in the Episcopal Church of USA, for the notion that women have an absolute right to be ordained seems to me as doubtful as the notion which has been held up till now that men have an inalienable right to the priesthood. For the very idea of excluding a class of persons is inconsistent with the truth that ordination is by grace and not by right or demand.

But the general emancipation of women is in accordance with God's will for freedom, and the church must naturally reflect this aspect of God's purposes in the ministry. But what is happening is not a change in the character of the ministry; it is simply filling up vacancies in it, and these have perhaps been implicit from the beginning, for instance in the ministry of the women to our Lord and the disciples. At that time it appeared primarily as 'diakonia'; today I believe it is apparent in the priesthood.

As I said in my Bishop's Charge to the diocese in 1971: 'What we are proposing is no deviation in Christian moral standards, no change in creed, no radical break with liturgical order. We remain firm in our love and loyalty to the Holy Catholic Church, which is our name "Sheng Kung Hui" in Chinese.'

This is not a party question, not a question of who is most clever in debate, not a question of mobilizing numbers or lobbying for votes. It is a matter which we should lay quietly before the Holy Spirit, not expecting an immediate or even perhaps a unanimous answer; but by opening our hearts to God, listening with imagination, and building on the experience we have, I believe the church will be guided step by step to the true fulness of its ministry.

CHAPTER 6

WHY NOT NOW?

MICHAEL PERRY

'How long, how long?' cried St Augustine in the garden, as he was struggling within himself and moving towards the final stage of his conversion. 'Tomorrow and tomorrow? Why not now?'

Anglicans who yearn for a decision by their church which will bring women into the priesthood may be forgiven for feeling very like Augustine. The road has been a long one. The Anglican Group for the Ordination of Women to the Historic Ministry of the Church has been campaigning for almost half a century, trying to build up an informed public opinion in favour of the move. It is over thirty-three years since the ordination of Florence Lee Tim Oi in war-time Hong Kong, though that caused so much embarrassment to so many people that she was persuaded to resign her orders after a couple of years.

The Hong Kong affair led the bishops at the 1948 Lambeth Conference to consider the matter. They replied firmly that even to experiment over a limited period 'would be against [Anglican] tradition and order and would gravely affect the internal and external relations of the Anglican Communion'.

The question, however, refused to go away. The Archbishops of Canterbury and York set up a Commission in 1962 whose report *Women and Holy Orders* was debated by Church Assembly in 1967. A motion which spoke of there being 'no conclusive theological reasons why women should not be ordained to the priesthood' and asked that the subject be further considered, passed the bishops and laity but was defeated in the House of Clergy. A further motion calling for women's vocations to be tested in the same way as men's was lost in all three houses, by an aggregate of 207 votes to 60.

In the following year the Lambeth Conference met again. A section report found 'no conclusive theological reasons for withholding ordination to the priesthood from women as such', but the full Conference was more guarded and would only grant that 'the theological arguments as at present presented for and against the ordination of women to the priesthood are inconclusive' and called for continuing study.

Events gained increasing momentum in the 1970s. Hong Kong again led the way by asking the Anglican Consultative Council what would happen if its bishop went ahead and ordained the two women candidates who were waiting for him to priest them. By 24 votes to 22 the Council said that such action would be acceptable to it and that it would use its good offices to encourage all provinces of the Anglican Communion to remain in communion with a diocese or province which acted in this way.

By 1973 the majority in the ACC had risen to 50 votes to 2 on the question of remaining in communion with a church which ordained women, and 54 to 1 on the view that although ecumenical considerations were important, they should not be decisive.

Discussion had now given place to action. By the end of 1977 women had been ordained priests in Hong Kong, the Anglican Church of Canada, the Episcopal Church of the USA and the Church of the Province of New Zealand. Other Anglican churches agree in principle but are not ready to take action. Amongst them are those in England (by an aggregate vote of 245 to 180 in General Synod on 3 July 1975, though the majority in the House of Clergy, at 110 to 96, was much narrower), Wales, Ireland, Australia, Burma, Kenya and the Indian Ocean. Synods in Central Africa, Singapore and Tanzania have voted against, and bishops and clergy in other provinces have voted to take no decision.

What lessons are there to be learnt from that whirlwind tour of Anglican progress over the last half-century?

1. The movement has undoubtedly gained momentum in the last decade, but we cannot accuse it of indecent haste. As Bishop Kenneth Woollcombe said to General Synod on 3 July 1975,

> I pause for a moment to address a word to those who think that we are being pressed to come to a hasty decision. The credal evolution of the doctrine of the Holy Spirit took place between the years 325 and 381, but most of the theological work on the doctrine was done during the last two decades of that half-century. The debate on the ordination of women began just after the First World War, but most of the significant theology has emerged during the last 20 years. The two periods are directly comparable in size and character, and do not support the view that we have been hastier than the Fathers.

2. Theological work has been done, and much of it has been done recently. The Lambeth Fathers may have been right to say in 1968 that 'the theological arguments as at present presented ... are inconclusive'. By 1975 that last adjective had become out of date and the Synod could rightly recognize that there were 'no fundamental objections'.

3. Anglican tradition is a developing thing. Lambeth in 1948 could speak of the move as against Anglican tradition, but in 1978 it will have to recognize that it has happened, as part of the developing tradition, in many Anglican churches and provinces. (Compare the way in which Lambeth's condemnatory attitude towards family planning in 1930 changed to the commendation in 1958 of its responsible exercise.) The declaration which, since 1975, clergy of the Church of England have had to make on ordination and on moving to a new appointment, speaks of doctrine in far less static terms than would have satisfied former generations. The church must

carefully, prayerfully and theologically assess what the secular world around is saying to it, because God can use even Cyrus (Isa. 45.1) as an agent of his purpose.

4. There appears to be a tide in the affairs of the Anglican Communion. We have not yet reached a consensus, but the general direction of the tide is incontrovertible. No one should claim any great significance in any single set of voting figures quoted above—in particular, it would be foolish to suggest that a vote of 110 to 96 in the House of Clergy of General Synod on 3 July 1975 showed that 'the Church of England has decided that there are no fundamental objections to women's ordination'. But the figures, and the way they change over the years, do suggest a pattern, and it is a pattern of a steadily developing movement in the direction of a much more substantial consensus. That is the way things work in the Anglican Communion. We do not wait for everybody to agree, or expect Lambeth to drill the squads into unanimity. Things take on, gradually—as, for example, revised liturgies are taking on in church after church of the Anglican Communion, not by Lambeth *fiat* but by local decision.

5. In this process, different parts of the world will move at different speeds, and no church ought to act until there is such a consensus that it would be more offensive to more people to refuse to act than to go forward. It would be folly to force women's ordination on a church that was not ready for it, and where women were not already being used (as servers, as Readers, as deaconesses, as leaders in the congregation) so extensively that the question of their ordination to the priesthood had begun to press intolerably hard on the consciousness of the church in question. So, by asking for the ordination of women now in the Church of England, we make no judgment on the fullness of the ministry of other churches in other parts of the world or in other centuries than our own. We do not say that the church was deficient in earlier centuries and that only today have we discovered what is necessary to give it the fullness of priesthood.

That would be arrogant indeed. What we do say is that we *become* deficient in our ministry if we refuse to widen it when the time is acceptable. In a moving situation, we cannot remain faithful by making an unchanging response. What it would have been wrong to do in 1280 it may be wrong *not* to do in 1980. As far as the Church of England is concerned, we are moving into a very crucial phase. The General Synod vote of 1975 did not reveal a sufficient consensus; the majority was so slender that the Synod was right to wait until the bishops decided the time was ripe to test the temperature of the water once more. By the end of 1978, three-and-a-half years after the former vote, in the light of Anglican developments in the interim, and taking account of what will have been said at the 1978 Lambeth Conference, we shall see how much further we are towards a consensus. Soon—and probably this time—it will be right for the English church to act. But first we must ask, (*i*) what can we learn from the experience of other parts of the world, and (*ii*) what are the ecumenical implications?

Women have been ordained elsewhere in the world, and we should learn from the experience of other countries. The State connexion of the Church of Sweden (where the first women were ordained in 1960) is so strong that the church was virtually coerced into having women priests as part of the movement towards equality of opportunity for women. The resultant rancour lasted a very long time indeed, and we may be thankful that in England the Sex Discrimination Act of 1975 specifically excluded the Churches from its provisions. Theological decisions with pastoral implications cannot be made under duress.

The unhappiness in Sweden was similar to that which is now racking the Episcopal Church in the USA (ECUSA), though in that case the pressure has been from within the church. What seems to happen in a church where the possibility of women's ordination is raised is that at first the thing is a remote and theoretical possibility, which does not touch many people because there seem to be few women with a claim to such a vocation. As the years go by and the number in favour of the move grows, the theoretical possibility begins to appear practicable and the tension mounts to a critical point. By the time the minority in favour has turned into a majority, it is hard not to be strident or uncharitable—whether one is for or against the proposal. Since the vocation to the priesthood is seen to be conceivable for women, there will be more women who will consider it seriously. More and more priests and bishops will be persuaded that it would be a right move to take, and become more and more unhappy not to be permitted to do what seems right. This is the stage which had been reached in ECUSA by 1974. Some women felt so strongly that they found retired bishops to perform quasi-ordinations without canonical authority. Some bishops declared they would ordain no more men as priests until they were allowed to ordain women as well. On the other side there were priests and laypeople who said that if the Episcopal Church ordained a single woman they could no longer conscientiously remain within its communion.

That was the hurtful situation before the 1976 General Convention of ECUSA. The question would not go away, and there was going to be distress whether the answer was 'yes' or 'no'—and 'not yet' would have made for even more intolerable tensions. In the event, as everybody knows, the General Convention said 'yes', the uncanonically ordained women's orders were regularized, and there have been several ordinations of women since.

The majority of congregations in ECUSA appear to be happy with the verdict, and those who would prefer not to have a woman minister realize that the few women who have been ordained will go to other congregations where they are welcome. Women will not be asked to serve where their ministry is unacceptable.

Others deplore the verdict and wish that it had gone the other way, yet wish to remain within ECUSA despite it all. The Presiding Bishop himself is of this opinion.

A very small—but vocal—minority has decided that the Episcopal Church is now no longer the church they knew. The ordination of women is for them the last straw. They had expressed disquiet about other tendencies in the church, such as the course of liturgical revision and the liberalizing views towards divorce and homosexuality which appeared to them to be taking a hold in ECUSA. They have therefore split away to form a body known as 'The Anglican Church in North America' which they claim is the true and unchanging ECUSA from which the main body has defected. Their first four bishops were consecrated on 28 January 1978, but they could only find two consecrating bishops rather than the normal minimum of three. One was a retired bishop of ECUSA and the other a bishop of the Philippine Independent Catholic Church (a body in full communion with all Anglican churches) who was acting without the knowledge or consent of his Supreme Bishop. It is sad to see those who champion Catholic order departing so quickly into petty sectarianism. The new church has already split in two over the propriety of the consecrations and the Archbishop of Canterbury and the Presiding Bishop of ECUSA refuse to recognize either of the two new churches. The dissidents number about ninety congregations—a tiny minority in a church of almost three million members.

The existence of 'The Episcopal Church in North America' is to be regretted but its importance in practical terms is minimal, and breakaway groups do not appear to have been formed elsewhere in Anglicanism where women are ordained. The auguries are that when women are ordained in the Church of England there will be a few people who will no longer be able to walk with us. That should not make us insensitive or uncaring, but when the time comes, we shall have reluctantly to say to them that the distress caused by refusal to act will be greater than that caused by acting. I believe that when the time comes, the majority will be in favour of women's ordination and that most of those who disagree will continue to do so *within* our communion and fellowship.*

Anglicanism is the least liable of all the great communions to schism, perhaps because the bounds of her doctrinal comprehensiveness are so widely drawn that it is hard to believe one's-self outside the pale. The same is true of the Anglican Communion as a body. So far, no church or province has withdrawn from communion with any Anglican church which ordains women, and the 1976 Anglican Consultative Council declared, without dissent, that in this matter 'the Anglican Communion faces an opportunity ... to give witness to diversity without breaking the bonds of love which bind us in one communion'. Intercommunion does not require prior agreement on every point.

There is one anomaly which has already made for difficulties, and that is that priests are no longer completely mutually interavailable throughout the Anglican Communion. What happens if a woman, validly and canonically ordained within her own province, goes to a province which will not ordain women? May she act as a priest there or not? The Central African Synod and the South Pacific Anglican Council have said that she will not be *persona grata* there, and the bishops of the Church of England have declared that they may not legally grant permission to any woman, however valid her ordination in her own church, to officiate in the provinces of Canterbury and York. This statement has not been debated in Synod or tested in the courts, and the point is not yet a sufficiently important one for Synod to spend time on it. But if the ordination of women in England is much longer delayed, the anomaly ought to be properly dealt with. It is at present an insult to any Church of the Anglican Communion which has tested the vocation of a

---

* In the province of New Zealand there were several threats of secession, if women were ordained, but none had materialized by February 1978. In one diocese the Vicar General, a leading opponent in earlier debates, presented the first women candidates to be ordained! (*Editor*)

woman and canonically ordained her, to say that a priest from that Church is unacceptable here for no other reason than that the Church of England has not yet made up her mind. We should extend to those from other cultures the rights they have in their own church and country as part of the courtesies of hospitality, even if in our own situation we are not able to go as far as they do—especially as our own Synod has declared that there is 'no fundamental objection' in principle.*

We must now move on to consider the ecumenical implications. The Ten Propositions of the Churches' Unity Commission (set out in January 1976) ask the English churches to declare their willingness to join in a covenant actively to seek visible unity. Proposition 6 makes it clear that the covenant would include the mutual recognition by all covenanting churches of each other's ordained ministries as true ministries of word and sacraments in the Holy Catholic Church.

The Baptist, Methodist and United Reformed Churches already ordain women ministers. If the Church of England were to enter the covenant, we would thereby accept them as true ministers of word and sacrament. General Synod will be asked in July 1978 to declare whether the Ten Propositions are a good enough basis for continued negotiations. By mid-February 1978, sixteen diocesan synods had debated the Propositions and fourteen of these had found them acceptable. (Of the remaining two, one had an aggregate vote of 107 to 15 in favour, but the motion failed as the Bishop voted against it.) It would be difficult to accept the propositions and enter into a covenant to recognize Free Church ministries, only to say that their male ministries alone were acceptable. The Church of England's failure to ordain women is

* In New Zealand the Bishop of Nelson has refused to authorize women priests to officiate in his diocese, although they have been canonically ordained in his province. This is the kind of stress which the Anglican Communion is already being called—successfully —to bear. (*Editor*)

already an obstacle to unity with the Free Churches, and it is not much more than fortuitous that so few of the officially-recognized Local Ecumenical Projects (formerly Areas of Ecumenical Experiment) have a woman Free Church minister on the staff who celebrates the eucharist for the Anglican members of the joint congregation (the author only knows of two such in the United Kingdom—Redditch and Livingston).

The Roman Catholic Bishops' Conference on 8 December 1977 declared that they could not accept Proposition 6 and that they would therefore be unable to enter into the proposed covenant. The Orthodox Church was not represented on the Churches' Unity Commission, and Archbishop Athenagoras has stated that the propositions 'cannot possibly be accepted. They cannot even be discussed by the Orthodox Church in England'. The difficulties felt by these two churches go far beyond the matter of women's ordination, but it is this on which we must concentrate for our present purposes.

The General Synod on 3 July 1975 asked the Archbishop of Canterbury to inform the appropriate authorities in the Roman Catholic and Orthodox Churches of its decision that there were 'no fundamental objections' to women's ordination, and to invite them to share in an urgent re-examination of the theological grounds for including women within the order of priesthood. The Pope replied that this was 'not admissible ... for very fundamental reasons' and that if Anglicans were to ordain women, it could not fail to introduce 'an element of grave difficulty' into Anglican–Roman dialogue, but that he believed that 'obstacles do not destroy mutual commitment to a search for reconciliation'.

The Sacred Congregation for the Doctrine of the Faith expanded the Pope's statement in *Inter insigniores*, a 'Declaration on the Question of the Admission of Women to the Ministerial Priesthood' which it published on 27 January 1977 together with an official commentary. Its tone was intransigent. The church 'does not consider herself authorized' to take this move; the question 'impinges too directly on the nature of the ministerial priesthood for one to agree that it should be resolved within the framework of legitimate pluralism between churches'.

The Orthodox reply was even less encouraging. The Archbishop's letter drew a reply from Archbishop Athenagoras of Thyateira and Great Britain, who made it clear that the Holy Synod would be entirely opposed to a move which stemmed from nothing more than 'contemporary fashion which overthrows the evangelical order and the experience of the Church'. At the Anglican–Orthodox Commission's meeting in Moscow in 1976 the Orthodox delegates left on record their belief that women's ordination 'will create a very serious obstacle to the development of our relations in the future'.

We must not forget that the Romans are in ecumenical dialogue with the Orthodox, and it may well be that the Pope does not wish to endanger the moves to heal the breach of 1054 by too close a rapprochement towards Protestantism.

To many Anglicans, these reactions of Rome and the Orthodox churches are crucial. By God's grace, the Church of England maintained through the Reformation the three-fold Catholic ministry and it would be a tragedy if we were to desert it now by admitting to the priesthood those whom Rome and the Orthodox aver are incapable of receiving the priestly character. Admittedly the Orthodox Church does not recognize our orders, and the Roman Catholic Church in 1896 declared them 'absolutely null and utterly void', but we have great hope in the present ecumenical climate that ways will be found of getting round this nineteenth-century intransigence. To move away from Rome would be to destroy all the ecumenical gains so hardly won in recent decades and to remove all hopes of mutual recognition of ministries. So crucial a move as the ordination of women could be made by no authority less than a fully ecumenical council representing both Rome and the Orthodox world, in which the context of decision-making would be the whole of the Christian world and any tendency to Western parochialism could be confined within the insights of churches in very different kinds of societies. Roman and Orthodox understandings of women (and the high place they give to the Mother of our Lord) ought to counterbalance the strident 'unisex' of English and American propaganda. According to the Vincentian Canon, what has been believed *semper et ubique et ab omnibus* cannot be set aside by one national church—and of this there is no clearer example than the maleness of the priesthood. If Anglicans claim a share in the priesthood of the universal church rather than a distinctively and parochially Anglican ministry, they cannot take action unilaterally on so central an issue.

That is a formidable list of objections, but it cannot close the case.

1. The Pope's letter to Archbishop Coggan, and the declaration *Inter insigniores*, are weighty documents of an authoritative nature, but they are not infallible. Already Fr John Wijngaards, Vicar General of the Mill Hill Fathers (in his book *Did Christ Rule Out Women Priests?*), has questioned both these documents, and does not cut himself off from communion with Rome by so doing. Theologians of the stature of Küng, Rahner, Daniélou and O'Collins believe that a woman's vocation to the priesthood ought to be tested in the same way as a man's, and the Alliance of St Joan has been working within the Roman Church since 1911 to this end. The Second Vatican Council declared that 'it is important that [women] participate more widely also in the various sectors of the Church's apostolate' and stated that 'forms of social and cultural discrimination in basic personal rights on the grounds of sex ... must be curbed and eradicated as incompatible with God's design. It is regrettable that these basic personal rights are not yet being respected everywhere, as is the case with women who are denied the chance freely to choose a ... state of life' (*The Church in the Modern World*, 29). Some Roman Catholics see *Inter insigniores* as a final authoritative word, but others believe it to be the last despairing

fling of the *vieux garde* of Roman traditionalists trying to do a Canute on the rising tide of the theological conviction that the Lord is calling his church to new adventures in a new age. It is still a *quaestio disputata* whether the maleness of priests is of the *esse* of the priesthood or is simply fortuitous, like the celibacy of the priesthood which, though a venerable tradition, could in principle be dispensed with. By joining the ranks of those Anglican churches which already ordain women, the Church of England might strengthen the hands of those Roman theologians and pastors and people who want to persuade their church to do the same.* They will have a hard struggle, as the tide in their church has not yet turned. Practically speaking, it is clear from recent events that full communion with Rome would only be possible if Anglicans were prepared to move closer to Rome than the Old Catholics—and that may serve to put the ecumenical argument against ordination of women in its right perspective. Ecumenical conversations will go on, but fresh items must be added to the dialogue.

2. Dialogue with the Orthodox must continue. The Joint Communiqué of the Oecumenical Patriarch and the Archbishop of Canterbury stated that 'the Anglican Church was not seeking the agreement of the Orthodox Church on this subject, but was hoping for understanding of it. The two leaders agree that the official dialogue between the Anglicans and Orthodox should continue'. It would be unrealistic to expect the Orthodox to accept even male Anglican orders at present, and the difference of ethos between the two churches is very considerable, as is obvious to the reader of the documents printed in *Anglican-Orthodox Dialogue* (SPCK, 1977). Tradition, for the Orthodox, is one and indivisible; it can develop, but it cannot contradict or go back on itself. In the continuing dialogue, each church will have to realize that the other holds a different view of how far and in what ways tradition is determinative of the issue. What is

* See Bishop Baker's account of the friendly welcome by Roman Catholics in Hong Kong to Anglican women priests, p. 71.

right and possible for some Anglican churches now, is clearly inconceivable to the Orthodox. Until they can grant that this is a matter on which autocephalous churches may hold different practices without mutual excommunication, we shall just have to agree to differ.

3. The role of the Blessed Virgin Mary in this matter seems to be a piece of double-think. She is a woman and has a very special place in the scheme of salvation. That her very existence lends an honour to womanhood which could not be enhanced by bestowal of the priesthood on any woman seems by no means to follow from that. Nor does there seem to be any relevance in the fact that she was not a disciple or apostle. To deny the priesthood to a woman on the grounds that our devotion to the Blessed Virgin Mary indicates sufficiently the honour paid to her sex as a whole, seems unjust and insensitive to the vocations of many women.

4. By seeking to open the priesthood to women, we do not drop our claim to be part of the universal ministry of the church catholic; we claim to be developing that ministry, under God's guidance, in new forms for a new age. *Inter insigniores* admits that 'we are dealing with a doctrine which classical theology scarcely touched upon', so the Vincentian Canon is irrelevant. Although the ministry has been confined to males *ubique et ab omnibus*, the *semper* part of the Canon only applies up till now, because only now has the time become ripe—and then only in certain societies—to carry out the theological examination.

5. To ask for the matter to be settled by a General Council is to cry for the moon. To be truly ecumenical it would need to include the churches of the Reformation as well as those of Rome and Orthodoxy. That might show up the Eastern parochialism of the Orthodox, who seem incapable of seeing things from a Western viewpoint! There is no practicable hope for an ecumenical council within the forseeable future; when General Councils cannot be called, decisions have to be made at a lower than conciliar level. This is what the Church of

Rome has done. Its dogmas (e.g. of infallibility in 1870, or of the Assumption in 1950) have been declared without waiting for the agreement of Canterbury or of Constantinople, let alone of Geneva. The Primate of the Anglican Church of Canada, Archbishop Scott, has pointed out that, historically speaking, General Councils did not initiate completely new courses of action in the church but confirmed some beliefs and practices which were under way and rejected others. 'In the early Church many things were tried in one area and then either approved or rejected for Catholic use. Perhaps, today, we need again to consider this as a valid way of acting.' Part of the sadness of schism is that in a divided church it may be necessary for a part to do what the whole is not yet prepared to do; but the action of a part may help the rest to come to its later decision more easily.

6. Finally, we as Anglicans must act as it seems theologically proper for us to act, as autocephalous churches, not looking over our shoulder at what would or would not be acceptable to churches with whom we are not yet in communion. If there is to be true ecumenical dialogue, it must be dialogue between churches which act on their convictions, not between churches which repress their convictions for fear of giving offence to each other. We must act in love for our separated brethren, but unless it is the truth as we see it that we speak in love, our love is no more than a sentimental fear of giving offence.

What will happen in the Church of England when we begin to ordain women as priests? I hope that we shall not move until the consensus is strong enough for us to do so in charity and without schism. I believe we are moving towards that time. I echo the words of the Bishop of Massachusetts, preaching on 15 October 1977 at the ordination of Nancy Sargent, when he said, 'Our task is to remain together as members of his body who belong to one another and who in patience and understanding (or at least attempting to understand) pray for one another, wish one another well in the Spirit and do all we can to support each other in responding to that spirit as we understand God, the Holy Spirit, is calling us. We may have different interpretations but we have one spirit and we belong to one body'.

At the beginning I expect to see a few women being ordained—no great rush, no 'monstrous regiment', no swamping of the priesthood by too many new recruits at a time. I see many of those whose ministry in a place as deaconess or lay worker or as teacher or as religious has been blessed and appreciated, going forward naturally and with the full backing of those amongst whom they have already been ministering. There are few enough women with vocations yet, and many enough places where they would be welcomed as priests with love and enthusiasm, to make it absolutely sure that no woman will go as a priest unless she is wanted there. We cannot tell precisely what gifts they will add to the priesthood, for we have not yet known them as priests. We do expect the priesthood to be enriched by them. They are not pretending to be men, or doing work which men can do. They are women, bringing their femininity to God within the priesthood and making their gifts available in it to the whole people of God.

As for the practical difficulties about which some people are making heavy weather, they will be solved as we go along—married women and children, 'difficult days', premenstrual tension, menopausal hang-ups. These are things the Free Churches with women ministers know about; and they have not found them insuperable.

In the Church of England, we stand in the valley of decision. With women amongst our priests, 'a great door and effectual' could be opened to us. If in the months ahead, we can come to a common mind, God will be able to do great things through a widened ministry. Let us not fail him, for now is the appointed time!